License to Cook Wisconsin §

Compiled by Juanita Loven

Wisconsin is an Indian word with several possible meanir
gathering of the water, wild rice country, and homelanc

Edited by Miriam Canter, Dorothy Crum, Michelle Nagle
Joan Liffring-Zug Bourret, and John Zug
Covers designed by Dana Lumby
Line drawings by Diane Heusinkveld

*Special thanks to the Wisconsin Department of Agriculture, the Wisconsin i
Board, the Bed and Breakfast Innkeepers, and other great cooks who s
recipes. (All other recipes are from Juanita Loven unless otherwise c*

Penfield's Books

Ethnic culture and recipes, regional cookbooks, and these popular
"Stocking Stuffer" spiral-bound cookbooks are specialties of Penfield Books.
For more information send $2.00 for a complete catalog.
Visit our website: www.penfieldbooks.com

ISBN 1-57216-027-6
Copyright 1996 Penfield Press

Penfield Books
215 Brown Street
Iowa City, Iowa 52245

Contents

About the Author

Dedicated to the author's mother, Leona Zeman of Melrose, and to her sister, the late Betty Schneider of Black River Falls, both wonderful Wisconsin cooks.

Juanita Zeman Loven grew up on a west-central Wisconsin dairy farm. "In the good old days" there were thresher crews to feed and many family gatherings with good food as a focal point. Juanita's mother encouraged her children to explore cooking at an early age. Fresh dairy products and home-grown vegetables were plentiful.

The Loven family spent most of their four children's growing up years in Stoughton and Watertown, Wisconsin, with many weekends and vacations spent exploring Wisconsin's treasures: parks, historic sites, and festivals.

After her husband's school administrative work took them to Iowa, Juanita completed her degree in public communications at Luther College in Decorah, Iowa, at age 51. She then founded a historic inn featuring Czech cuisine in Spillville, Iowa. Juanita promotes tourism, advocates life-long learning, and keeps in touch with a growing number of grandchildren in Colorado, Maryland, and New York.

The Badger State

Wisconsin was nicknamed "The Badger State" because the first Wisconsin lead miners lived in caves dug out of the hillsides, reminding people of badgers.

In the 1600s Wisconsin's first white explorer, Frenchman Jean Nicolet, landed in Green Bay, seeking a water route to China! He found the area inhabited by Winnebago, Dakota, and Menominee tribes who fished, hunted, and grew corn, beans, and squash. Later Native American tribes included the Chippewa, Sauk, Fox, Ottawa, Kickapoo, Huron, Miami, Illinois, and Potawatomi. After various French and Native American skirmishes and treaties, Great Britain established claim to the territory. In 1774 English fur traders took over the fur trading posts.

From 1820 to 1830 Mineral Point was being settled by lead miners. The Erie Canal opened in 1825, making the Great Lakes an important immigrant route and contributing to the settling of Milwaukee. In 1830 Wisconsin was still a fur trading and military frontier. The tribes' last stand against the settlers was in 1832.

(continued)

The Badger State   *(continued)*

1830 through 1920 set Wisconsin's course toward becoming an agricultural state with urban centers growing along the lakes and rivers. Green Bay and Prairie du Chien were the first communities settled.

The food industry, which began with bartering with the Native Americans in the 1600s, grew to be Wisconsin's biggest business by 1850, two years after the territory became a state. At that time, one-third of the state's population was made up of immigrants from England, Canada, Switzerland, Germany, France, Ireland, Wales, The Netherlands, Norway, Denmark, Holland, Poland, and others—with Germans and Scandinavians playing a significant role.

Homesteaders planted gardens; they raised livestock and poultry, milked the cows, churned butter, and gathered the eggs. Family records of one of our editors reveal that a "clutch of turkeys" hatched aboard a steamship en route to a homestead

6

(continued)

in the Lake Pepin area. Native Americans exchanged wild rice, corn, and game for dairy products. By the 1890s the dairy farm was clearly established.

Today manufacturing accounts for over 30% of the gross state product. The chief products, in order of importance are: non-electronic machinery, food products, paper products, fabricated metal products, and transportation equipment.

Tourists love discovering the beauty of the state. The glaciers gave the Wisconsin landscape its gently rolling, smoothly rounded appearance as well as dug out the Great Lakes, smaller lakes, and rivers. Melting glaciers left large boulders, rocks, depressions—"kettles" and "potholes." The beautifully carved gorge of the Wisconsin River at the Dells was produced when a glacier changed the course of the river, and in melting caused great volumes of rapidly moving water to cut a deep channel in the rock—also sculpting many odd rock formations. Fertile farm lands add to the wonders of the natural beauty of Wisconsin.

Exploring Wisconsin

Take advantage of Wisconsin's natural beauty and exciting and unique attractions—from the urban beat of the great cities to the quiet retreat in the north woods.

Try deep-water sport fishing on the Great Lakes. Splash through a waterfall. Drop a line in a trout stream or try your luck at hunting (in season, of course). Enjoy boating, water-skiing, and fishing in one of 15,000 inland glacial lakes. Ride an inner tube down the Apple River. Canoe the "crookedest river in the world, " the Kickapoo River. Raft the Lower Wolf River. Ride the rapids or cruise the Mississippi on a houseboat or paddle wheeler. Camp in one of many private or state-owned parks, forests, or recreational areas. Follow Wisconsin roads to restored frontier villages, intriguing craft shops, and circus, railroad, and maritime museums. Watch birds in a variety of settings. Tour a dairy farm. Stay at a bed and breakfast inn. Ride a camel, a ferry, or a steam train. Golf some of the nation's most beautiful courses. Hike the Ice Age Trail—including 830 miles of marked trails and 60 miles

8

(continued)

Exploring Wisconsin *(continued)*

of nature trails through state parks and public preserves. Bike over 300 miles of the finest off-road trails. Attend a ball game, art fair, symphony, or auto race. Discover some of the best botanical gardens, zoos, and museums. Dine on local specialties. Enjoy skiing, skating, snowmobiling, and tobogganing in season. See cheese being made, beer brewed, and cranberries harvested. Join in the fun at festivals across the state celebrating ethnic heritage, community tradition, and the change of seasons.

Wisconsin abounds in preservation of nature, with 49 state parks, 10 state trails, three national parks, and nine national forests. Twenty picturesque islands on an 11-mile strip of the Bayfield Peninsula along the south shore of Lake Superior comprise The Apostle Islands National Lakeshore. A 27-mile segment along the lower St. Croix River provides recreational opportunities for much of the upper Midwest. Another 200 miles of the St. Croix and its Namekagon tributary make up an additional National Scenic River area. Chequamegon National Forest (north central) has 170 lakes. Nicolet National Forest (northeast) has 260 lakes.

Wisconsin Foods

Wisconsin is America's dairyland. The state produces 17% of the nation's milk, 35% of the cheese, 25% of the butter, and a large variety of milk by-products. Dairying provides almost 60% of Wisconsin's agricultural income. There are approximately 4.4 million cattle in the state—one for every person.

Diversity is a key element in the state's agricultural economy. Wisconsin is first in the production of corn for silage, snap beans, sweet corn, and cabbage for sauerkraut; second in cranberries and peas; third in sausage; among the top 10 in output of tart cherries, mint, potatoes, oats, corn for grain, hay, cattle, honey, carrots, and cucumbers.

Wisconsin is also a leader in beer production with Milwaukee as the center. There are recipes utilizing beer throughout this book.

Add one of Wisconsin's 170 kinds of fish to the variety of homegrown dairy, meat, and vegetable products, and you have a bounty of food choices fit for royalty! The recipes in the book make use of the wealth of Wisconsin products.

Appetizers and Beverages

Appetizers:

Cheddar Butter Spread	12
Cheese Pretzels	13
Czech Pickled Pork Hocks	14
Dairyland Dipper	15
French-Fried Cheese	16
Vegetables in Wisconsin Beer Batter	17
Wisconsin Cheese Wheel	18

Beverages:

Cherry Bounce	19
Cranberry Cocktail	20
Holiday Punch	20
Rhubarb Shrub	21

Robin
Wisconsin State Bird

Cheddar Butter Spread

Wisconsin Milk Marketing Board, Madison, Wisconsin

4 ounces shredded Wisconsin
  Cheddar cheese
1/2 cup butter, softened
1 clove garlic, minced
  or 1/8 teaspoon garlic powder

1 teaspoon lemon juice
1/2 teaspoon basil
1/4 teaspoon thyme
1/8 teaspoon pepper

In a small bowl, combine all ingredients. Blend until smooth and fluffy. Serve in a crock or roll into a 12-inch log, 1 1/2 inches in diameter. Cover and refrigerate. Remove from refrigerator 20 to 30 minutes before serving. Serve with bread, vegetables, or meats. Makes 1 cup.

Cheese Pretzels

A good family activity.

1 package dry yeast
1 tablespoon sugar
1 1/2 cups warm water
1 teaspoon salt

4 to 5 cups flour, divided
1 pound sharp Cheddar cheese, grated
1 egg, beaten
coarse salt

Dissolve yeast and sugar in water. In a large bowl, combine salt with 4 cups of the flour and the cheese. Stir in the yeast mixture, adding more flour if needed to form a stiff dough. Knead for 5 to 10 minutes, until smooth. Break off small pieces of dough, about walnut size. Roll into a thin rope, then twist and loop the rope into a traditionally shaped pretzel or your own design. Place on an ungreased baking sheet, allowing room for expansion. Brush each with beaten egg and sprinkle lightly with coarse salt. Bake at 425° for 15 to 18 minutes, or until golden brown. The number of pretzels depends on size preferred and each person's creativity.

Czech Pickled Pork Hocks

Catherine Hynek, Hillsboro, Wisconsin

4 pork hocks, split on sides
2 to 3 quarts water
2 tablespoons salt

1 onion, diced
2 whole allspice
pepper
1 cup vinegar

In a large pot, combine pork hocks with enough water to cover, salt, onion, and allspice. Boil until very tender. Cool, debone, and dice pork hocks. Strain the broth and add plenty of pepper, the vinegar, and the diced meat. Heat until heated through. Pour into a crock and add water to cover meat. Set aside to congeal, usually overnight. Slice and serve cold.

Note: Other cuts of pork may be used with Knox gelatin.

Dairyland Dipper
Wisconsin Department of Agriculture

2 8-ounce packages cream cheese
1 pound Cheddar cheese, grated
2/3 cup sour cream
4 teaspoons prepared horseradish

2 tablespoons grated onion
10 slices bacon, cooked and crumbled
1 14-inch or 3 4-inch round loaves
   pumpernickel or rye bread
crackers and fresh cut vegetables

Combine cheeses, sour cream, horseradish, onion, and bacon in a blender. Blend until smooth. Cut a slice from the top of the loaf and hollow out the center, forming a bowl. Cut the bread from the center into cubes and place on an ungreased baking sheet. Bake at 375° for 10 minutes or until toasted. Fill the pumpernickel or rye bowls with the cheese mixture. Serve with the bread cubes, crackers, and fresh vegetable dippers. Serves 15 to 20.

15

French-Fried Cheese

Wisconsin Department of Agriculture

2 pounds Cheddar, Muenster,
brick, or Colby cheese cut
into 1/2-inch cubes

2 eggs, beaten
seasoned dry bread crumbs or flour
vegetable oil

Dip each cheese cube in egg; coat with crumbs; repeat. Heat oil to 350° to 375°; fry cheese in hot oil until lightly browned. Serve immediately.

Note: Cheese curds may be substituted for cheese cubes. Cheese may also be coated ahead of time and refrigerated until ready to fry.

Vegetables in Wisconsin Beer Batter

1 1/3 cups flour
2 tablespoons Parmesan cheese
1 tablespoon chopped parsley
1 teaspoon salt
dash of garlic

12-ounce can Wisconsin beer, at
    room temperature and flat
2 eggs, separated
green peppers, cauliflower, onion,
    artichoke hearts, zucchini, or
    broccoli, cut into bite-sized pieces
oil for deep frying

In a large bowl, combine flour, cheese, parsley, salt, and garlic. Stir in the beer and egg yolks. Beat egg whites until stiff and fold into beer mixture. Dip vegetable pieces into batter. Heat oil to 375° and fry a few pieces of batter-dipped vegetables at a time in oil until golden. Drain on paper toweling. Serve immediately.

Wisconsin Cheese Wheel

Wisconsin Milk Marketing Board

12 ounces Wisconsin Cheddar cheese, shredded
4 ounces Wisconsin Swiss cheese, shredded
8 ounces cream cheese, softened
1/2 cup mayonnaise
1/4 cup finely chopped onion
2 tablespoons finely chopped green pepper
2 teaspoons Worcestershire sauce
1 each: red, yellow, and green apples, cut into thin wedges, rinsed in slightly salted water to prevent discoloring
assorted crackers

In a large bowl, combine all ingredients except apples and crackers; mix well. Line the bottom of a 9-inch round cake pan with waxed paper. Press cheese mixture firmly into pan and refrigerate for several hours or until firm. Run a knife around the side of the pan; invert onto a serving platter. Remove waxed paper. Arrange apple slices decoratively on top and base of the cheese wheel. Serve with assorted crackers. Makes 5 cups.

Cherry Bounce

Country Ovens, Ltd., P.O. Box 195, Forestville, Wisconsin

Traditionally, Bounce is made from fresh cherries at harvest and uncorked for the first time during the holiday season. In 1987 Country Ovens, Ltd. started dehydrating cherries and found them superb. They decided everyone should enjoy cherries year-round. Cherry De-Lites are produced exclusively from the famous Door County, Wisconsin, grade "A" fancy cherries.

1 cup Cherry De-Lites* (dried cherries)
1 cup sugar or honey
1 tablespoon allspice
1 tablespoon whole cloves
1 stick cinnamon
1 quart whiskey or brandy

Fill a largemouth jar or wine jug with Cherry De-Lites, sugar, and spices. Add whiskey or brandy. Cork and let stand in a dark place for 2 months or more. The longer it ages the better it is. Strain before serving as a liqueur. Use the Cherry De-Lites for hors d'oeuvres.

*Cherry De-Lites are available from Country Ovens, Ltd. Address above.

Cranberry Cocktail

Lac du Flambeau Chamber of Commerce

2 cups cranberries
2 cups water

1/4 cup lemon juice
1/4 cup orange juice
1/2 to 1 cup sugar to taste

Cook berries in water until soft. Strain, then bring the liquid to a boil. Add juices and sweeten to taste. Stir until sugar is dissolved and chill. Makes about 4 cups.

Holiday Punch

2 cups cranberry cocktail
6 cups orange juice

3 cups ginger ale
2 10-ounce packages frozen
    strawberries, undrained

Prepare 2 cups of cranberry cocktail and add to the remaining holiday punch ingredients. Serve over ice. Serves 18.

Rhubarb Shrub

Mary Margaret Endres, Mineral Point, Wisconsin

1 quart finely chopped rhubarb
1 quart water
1 1/2 cups sugar
1/3 cup orange juice

4 tablespoons lemon juice
dash salt
crushed ice
soda water or ginger ale

Cook rhubarb in water until soft. Strain and add sugar to the rhubarb juice, stirring to dissolve. Add orange and lemon juices, and salt. Chill. Place 1/2 cup in a tall glass with crushed ice; fill with soda or ginger ale. Serves 10.

Soups, Stews, and Chowders

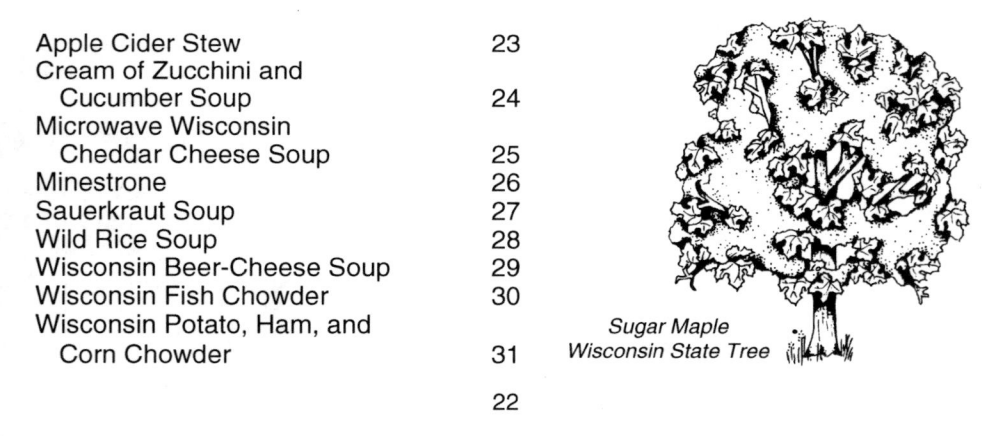

Sugar Maple
Wisconsin State Tree

Apple Cider Stew

3 tablespoons flour
2 teaspoons salt
1/4 teaspoon pepper
1/4 teaspoon thyme
2 pounds beef stew meat
3 tablespoons corn oil
2 cups apple cider

1/2 cup water
2 tablespoons vinegar
4 medium-sized carrots, quartered
3 medium-sized potatoes, peeled and diced
2 medium-sized onions, diced
1 stalk celery, cut in 1-inch pieces
1 apple, cored and diced

In a paper bag, combine flour, salt, pepper, and thyme. Add meat and shake to coat. In a Dutch oven, cook meat in hot oil until browned. Add cider, water, and vinegar. Bring to a boil; reduce heat and simmer for 1 1/2 to 2 hours or until meat is tender. Add remaining ingredients and cook for 30 minutes or until vegetables are tender. Serves 6.

Cream of Zucchini and Cucumber Soup

3 medium-sized zucchini, sliced
1 medium-sized cucumber,
  seeded and drained
3 stalks celery, sliced
2 scallions including greens,
  sliced

3 cloves garlic, minced
4 to 5 cups chicken broth
fresh herbs in season: parsley,
  dill, thyme, etc.
salt and pepper to taste
1 cup heavy cream, sour cream, or
  evaporated milk

Simmer zucchini, cucumber, celery, scallions, and garlic in broth with herbs until soft. Purée mixture in a blender or food processor in batches. Season to taste and stir in the cream. Serves 6. Delicious warm or cold.

Note: For texture, add some chopped raw zucchini or cucumber.

Microwave Wisconsin Cheddar Cheese Soup

Wisconsin Milk Marketing Board, Madison, Wisconsin

3 tablespoons butter
1/2 cup finely chopped green pepper
1/2 cup finely chopped celery
1/2 cup finely chopped carrots
1/2 cup finely chopped onion

4 cups chicken broth, divided
1/2 cup flour
1/2 pound Wisconsin mild
Cheddar cheese, grated
1/2 pound Wisconsin aged
Cheddar cheese, grated

In a 3-quart casserole, combine butter, green pepper, celery, carrots, onion, and 1/2 cup broth. Microwave, covered, on full power for 6 to 8 minutes or until vegetables are tender. Whisk flour into remaining broth; stir into vegetable mixture. Microwave, uncovered, on full power for 8 to 10 minutes until mixture thickens. Stir in cheese. Microwave on medium power for 10 minutes or until heated through, stirring once during the cooking time. Serves 8.

Minestrone

1 pound beef round, or chuck roast,
cut in 1/2-inch cubes
1 medium-sized onion, chopped
2 tablespoons vegetable oil
2 1/2 cups water
2 cans (10 1/2-ounces) beef broth
1 can (16-ounces) tomatoes in juice
1 bay leaf
1/2 teaspoon each celery salt,
onion powder

1/4 teaspoon each thyme, basil
1/8 teaspoon oregano
1 cup uncooked macaroni shells
1 can (16-ounces) mixed vegetables
1 can (10 1/2-ounces) dark red
kidney beans, rinsed and drained
1/2 package (10 ounces) frozen
chopped spinach
1/4 cup grated Parmesan cheese

In a large saucepan brown beef with onion in oil. Add water, broth, tomatoes, and seasonings. Bring to a boil; reduce heat; simmer 1 hour. Add macaroni and simmer 5 minutes. Add mixed vegetables, beans, and spinach; simmer 5 to 10 minutes more. Stir in Parmesan cheese just before serving. Yields 10 one-cup servings.

Sauerkraut Soup

2 large onions, coarsely chopped
1 stalk celery, diced
1/4 cup butter
1 1/2 pounds sauerkraut, rinsed
  and drained
10 cups beef broth
2 pounds lean beef, cubed

5 peppercorns
1 bay leaf
pinch thyme
small piece cheesecloth
salt and pepper to taste
6 to 8 small red potatoes, unpeeled
finely chopped dill
sour cream

In a large kettle, cook onion and celery in butter until tender. Add sauerkraut and cook over low heat until golden. Add beef broth and beef. Tie peppercorns, bay leaf, and thyme in cheesecloth; add to broth. Season to taste. Cook soup, covered, over low heat for at least 2 hours. About 20 to 30 minutes before serving; add the potatoes and cook until potatoes are tender. Remove cheesecloth bag of herbs. Serve soup sprinkled with finely chopped dill and sour cream on the side. Serves 6 to 8.

Wild Rice Soup

Lac du Flambeau Chamber of Commerce

2 tablespoons butter
1 tablespoon minced onion
1/4 cup chopped celery
1/2 cup sliced mushrooms
1/4 cup flour

4 cups chicken broth
2 cups cooked wild rice
salt and pepper to taste
1 cup cream

Melt butter and sauté onion, celery, and mushrooms. Blend in flour and add broth. Stir and cook until thick. Stir in rice and season to taste with salt and pepper. Simmer about 5 minutes. Blend in cream, but do not boil; heat to serving temperature.
Note: To cook wild rice: Put 1 cup rice and 3 cups boiling water in a saucepan with a tight-fitting lid. Reduce heat; simmer 30 to 45 minutes or until rice is tender. Drain. (One cup uncooked wild rice yields 3 to 4 cups.)

Wisconsin Beer-Cheese Soup

1 clove garlic, minced, optional
1/4 cup butter
1 cup flour
1/2 teaspoon paprika
salt and pepper to taste
6 cups chicken broth or part
  broth and part milk*

1/2 cup finely chopped onion
1/2 cup finely chopped mushrooms
  or celery
1/2 cup grated carrots
1/2 pound Wisconsin Cheddar
  cheese, grated
3 cups Wisconsin beer at room temperature

Sauté garlic in butter. Sprinkle with flour, paprika, salt, and pepper and cook until bubbly and golden. Gradually add broth. (If using part broth and part milk, add milk with the beer.) Bring broth mixture to a boil, stirring constantly. Reduce heat and add vegetables. Simmer for 20 minutes; do not boil. Add cheese and beer. Heat until hot but not boiling. Serves 8.
*Do not boil milk.

Wisconsin Fish Chowder

Janice Runge, Merrill, Wisconsin

2 to 4 slices bacon, cut into
  1-inch pieces
1 1/2 cups peeled, diced potatoes
1/3 cup diced onion
1/2 teaspoon salt

1/8 teaspoon pepper
1/2 cup water
1 pound fish (pike, coho, or lake trout)
3 cups milk
1 tablespoon chopped fresh parsley

Fry the bacon until golden. Add potatoes, onion, salt, pepper, and water. Cook, covered, over moderate heat for 5 to 10 minutes. Debone fish and cut into bite-sized pieces. Add fish and continue cooking, covered, over moderate heat for 8 to 12 minutes or until fish flakes and potatoes are tender. Add the milk and heat through, do not boil. Serve garnished with parsley. Serves 4.

Wisconsin Potato, Ham, and Corn Chowder

Wisconsin Potato Growers' Auxiliary

4 medium-sized Wisconsin potatoes
2 tablespoons butter
1/4 cup chopped onion
1/4 cup chopped green pepper
2 1/3 cups water, divided
1 teaspoon salt
1/8 teaspoon pepper
1/4 teaspoon paprika
3 tablespoons flour
2 cups milk
1 can (12 ounces) whole kernel corn
  with liquid
1 1/2 cups diced cooked ham
chopped parsley for garnish

Peel and dice potatoes. In a large saucepan melt butter; add onion and green pepper. Cook until tender. Add potatoes, 2 cups water, and seasonings. Cover and simmer until potatoes are tender. Make a paste of flour and remaining water; add to potato mixture. Then add milk and cook until slightly thickened; add corn and diced ham and heat through, stirring thoroughly. Sprinkle with parsley before serving. Makes about 6 servings.

Salads and Dressings

Apple Chicken Salad

Wisconsin Department of Agriculture

1 1/2 cups diced Wisconsin apples
1 cup cooked, diced chicken, chilled
1/2 cup sliced celery
1/4 cup pitted, sliced black olives

1/4 cup mayonnaise
2 tablespoons sour cream
1/4 teaspoon ground rosemary
1/4 teaspoon curry powder
crisp salad greens

Core and dice apples. In a large bowl, combine apples, chicken, celery, and olives. In a small bowl, combine mayonnaise, sour cream, rosemary, and curry powder. Add mayonnaise mixture to apple mixture and toss to coat. Line a serving bowl with salad greens and pour salad over greens. Serves 4 to 6.

Cottage Cheese Slaw

Watertown Memorial Hospital Kitchen, Watertown, Wisconsin

lettuce or other greens
1 cup cottage cheese, well drained
3 cups shredded green cabbage
1/2 cup shredded carrots
1/4 cup chopped green pepper
1 teaspoon chopped onion
1/2 cup mayonnaise

1 tablespoon half-and-half
1 tablespoon vinegar
1 teaspoon sugar
1 teaspoon salt
1/4 teaspoon pepper
paprika

Wash and chill greens to a crisp. In a large bowl, combine cottage cheese, cabbage, carrots, green pepper, and onion. In a small bowl, combine mayonnaise, half-and-half, vinegar, sugar, salt, and pepper. Pour over cottage cheese mixture and toss to coat. Arrange over greens and garnish with paprika. Serves 6.

Cranberry Sunset Salad

2 3-ounce packages red gelatin
2 cups hot water

2 cups whole cranberry sauce
1 cup sour cream
1 cup cottage cheese

Dissolve gelatin in hot water. Cool and add remaining ingredients and whip until thoroughly mixed. Pour into a 1 1/2-quart mold and chill. Serves 12.

Cucumber Salad

1 cup plain yogurt
2 tablespoons oil
4 teaspoons lemon juice

2 tablespoons fresh snipped mint
2 cups thinly sliced cucumbers
lettuce, optional

In a small bowl, stir together yogurt, oil, lemon juice, and mint. Add to sliced cucumber; toss to coat. Cover and chill. Serve cucumber mixture in a lettuce-lined salad bowl, if desired. Serves 4.

Note: This is a good stuffing for fresh tomatoes. Cut a hollow in the stem end of medium-sized tomatoes; salt and place on a rack to drain before filling with the cucumber salad.

Dairyland Summer Salad

1/2 cup sour cream
1/2 cup mayonnaise
1/2 cup shell macaroni
1/2 pound lean ground beef
salt and pepper to taste

Topping:
1 cup cottage cheese
1 cup plain yogurt

3 cups torn fresh spinach
1/2 cup sliced radishes
1/2 cup sliced celery
2 green onions, chopped
1/2 cup cucumber, sliced
1 1/2 cups shredded Cheddar cheese

salt and pepper to taste
6 slices bacon, cooked and crumbled
2 tablespoons minced parsley

(continued)

Dairyland Summer Salad   *(continued)*

Mix sour cream and mayonnaise; set aside. Cook macaroni according to package directions until almost done; drain, rinse, and chill. Brown beef and season to taste. Drain and cool. In a large bowl, combine macaroni, browned beef, vegetables, and cheese. Add sour cream mixture and toss to coat. Pour into a serving dish and top with the topping.

Topping: In a blender, combine cottage cheese, yogurt, salt, and pepper. Blend until smooth. Pour over salad. Cover and chill for 1 hour. Sprinkle with bacon and parsley. Serves 4.

Note: Diced roast beef, turkey, chicken, or ham may be substituted for ground beef.

Jellied Beet Salad

1 cup beets, peeled and diced
1 3-ounce package lemon gelatin
1 cup boiling water
3/4 cup beet juice
3 tablespoons cider vinegar

1/2 teaspoon salt
2 tablespoons grated onion
1 tablespoon grated horseradish
3/4 cup chopped celery
mayonnaise or your favorite dressing

Cook beets until tender; drain, reserving 3/4 cup juice. Dissolve gelatin in boiling water. Add beet juice and chill to thicken before adding beets and remaining ingredients, except mayonnaise or dressing. Pour into mold and chill until well set. Unmold and serve with mayonnaise or your favorite dressing. Serves 4.

Lo-Cal Yogurt Potato Salad

1 cup plain yogurt
2 teaspoons prepared mustard
2 teaspoons Wisconsin horseradish
2 cups cooked, cubed potatoes

1/2 cup sliced celery
1 medium-sized cucumber, sliced
1/4 cup sliced onion
1 teaspoon chopped chives

In a large bowl, combine yogurt, mustard, and horseradish. Add remaining ingredients and toss to coat. Refrigerate until cold. Serves 8.

Note: 60 calories per serving. The calorie count will change slightly, but for a less tart flavor, add 1/2 teaspoon sugar to the yogurt.

Macaroni Salad

2 cups uncooked elbow macaroni
1 cup cooked, cubed ham or sausage
1 cup sliced zucchini
1 cup chopped, pared cucumber

1 1/2 cups chopped tomato
1 cup sliced radishes
1/2 cup grated carrot (thin, wide grate)
1 cup creamy dill dressing (p. 45)
  or a dressing of choice

Cook macaroni until tender according to directions for kind used. Drain and cool. Combine meat and vegetables with macaroni; chill thoroughly. Toss with the dressing before serving. Makes 6 to 8 servings.

Marinated Field Lettuce and Chicken Salad

Chef Lewis, The American Club, Kohler, Wisconsin

1/2 pound spinach leaf, stemmed
and washed
1 head radicchio
6 sprigs watercress
1 head red leaf lettuce
Vinaigrette:
3/4 cup oil
1/4 cup vinegar
2 tomatoes, peeled, seeded, diced

6 field mushrooms, sliced
2 carrots, cut julienne
chicken breast, marinated, grilled,
and sliced

3 shallots, chopped
fresh herbs to taste
salt and pepper

Combine all vinaigrette ingredients. Wash and clean all greens. Drain thoroughly.
Toss greens with vinaigrette; arrange on plates. Arrange sliced mushrooms, carrot,
and chicken breast on top of the greens. Sprinkle with vinaigrette. Serves 6.

Beer Dressing for Potato Salad

Heileman Brewing Company, La Crosse, Wisconsin

1/2 cup diced onion
3 tablespoons salad oil
2 tablespoons flour
1 1/2 teaspoons salt

1/8 teaspoon pepper
2 teaspoons sugar
1 1/2 cups Old Style Beer
1/4 cup cider vinegar

Sauté the onion in oil for 10 minutes, stirring frequently. Blend in the flour, salt, pepper, and sugar. Gradually add the beer and vinegar, stirring constantly to the boiling point. Cook over low heat 5 minutes. Cool slightly and pour over prepared potatoes (cooked and sliced or diced). Makes about 1 3/4 cups.

German Potato Salad

2 pounds boiled potatoes, peeled
    and sliced

bacon drippings
1/2 pound bacon, fried and crumbled

Follow recipe for beer dressing, but use bacon drippings in place of oil and add crumbled bacon when mixing salad. Serve warm.   43

Cottage Cheese Dressing

1 cup cottage cheese
2 tablespoons mayonnaise

1 teaspoon Worcestershire sauce
1/4 teaspoon paprika
salt and pepper

In a small bowl, combine all ingredients and mix well. Makes 1 cup.

Cottage Cheese Fruit Dressing

1/2 cup cottage cheese
1/2 cup cream
1/2 cup lemon juice
dash of paprika

1/2 teaspoon salt
1 tablespoon honey or sugar
1 tablespoon chopped chives

In a small bowl, beat all ingredients together until smooth. Makes 1 1/3 cups.

Cottage Cheese Vegetable Dressing

1 cup cottage cheese
2 tablespoons vinegar
3 tablespoons sugar

1/4 teaspoon salt
1/4 teaspoon paprika
1/4 teaspoon prepared mustard
4 tablespoons ketchup

Combine all ingredients and mix well. Makes about 1 cup.

Creamy Dill Dressing

1/2 cup plain yogurt
1/2 cup cottage cheese
1/4 to 1/2 teaspoon minced garlic

1 tablespoon minced fresh dill
1 tablespoon olive oil
1/2 teaspoon fresh lemon juice

Place all ingredients into a blender or food processor. Mix until smooth. Makes about 1 cup.

Horseradish Vinaigrette

Silver Spring Gardens, Inc., Eau Claire, Wisconsin

Silver Spring Gardens, Inc. is a family-owned farm in northern Wisconsin that has been browning and bottling horseradish for over 60 years.

1 cup oil
1 tablespoon Silver Spring
  Dijon-style mustard
1/2 cup vinegar
1/4 cup sugar

2 teaspoons Silver Spring
  prepared horseradish
1 teaspoon lemon juice
1 clove garlic, crushed
1 teaspoon salt

Place all ingredients in a blender and blend until smooth. Makes about 2 cups. Good with mixed greens, raw vegetables, and pasta salads.
Note: Horseradish is especially good combined with balsamic vinegar in salad dressings and marinades.

Maple Fruit Mate

Wisconsin Maple Producers' Council

1 cup cottage cheese   4 tablespoons real maple syrup
1 tablespoon mayonnaise

Combine all ingredients in a blender. Cover and blend until smooth. May be used as a fruit dip or as a topping for a fruit salad.

Maple Syrup
Maple syrup is a north-woods trick
Just a spout, a bucket, and away it drips
It's a natural product, boiled down to a sweet
On pancakes or ice cream it's a real treat!
Taste for yourself and see
It's *"Something Special from Wisconsin"* and from our state tree.
Wisconsin Maple Producers' Council, Aniwa, Wisconsin

Breads, Muffins, Granola, Toppings, and Pancakes

Banana Sour Cream Coffee Cake

Penny Dunbar, The "Gables" Bed and Breakfast, Kewaunee, Wisconsin

2 cups flour
1 cup white sugar
1 teaspoon baking powder
1 teaspoon baking soda
1/2 teaspoon salt
1/2 teaspoon cinnamon
2 eggs
1 teaspoon vanilla

1/2 cup sour cream
1 cup mashed bananas
1/2 cup butter, softened
1/2 cup raisins, dried Door County
   cherries, or dried Wisconsin cranberry
   chips
powdered sugar for topping

Combine all ingredients except powdered sugar and mix until well blended. Pour into a well-greased Bundt pan. Bake at 350° for 45 minutes. Cool 5 minutes before removing from pan. Sprinkle with powdered sugar and serve warm. Serves 16.

Beer-Cheese Bread with Raisins

Pabst Brewing Company

A sweet, moist quick bread to serve for breakfast or with afternoon tea.

1 cup raisins (5 ounces)
1 can or bottle (12 ounces) beer
2 1/2 cups all-purpose flour
3/4 cup sugar
1 tablespoon baking powder
1/2 teaspoon baking soda

1/2 teaspoon salt
4 ounces Cheddar cheese,
  finely shredded
1/4 cup oil
1 egg

Heat raisins and beer to simmering. Remove from heat; let stand about 10 minutes. Combine dry ingredients. Add cheese; stir to coat. Mix oil and egg; add to dry ingredients along with beer and raisins. Beat just until blended. Turn into greased and floured 5x9x3-inch loaf pan. Bake at 350° for 1 hour. Turn out on a rack to cool. Cool thoroughly before slicing. Makes 1 loaf.

Cheese Popovers

Patricia Barnes, The Inn at Wildcat Mountain, Bed and Breakfast, Ontario, Wisconsin, says, "These popovers are wonderful with fruit for breakfast."

1 cup flour	2 eggs, beaten
1/2 teaspoon salt	1 tablespoon butter, melted
1 teaspoon sugar, optional	1/2 cup grated Wisconsin cheese,
1 cup milk	Swiss, Cheddar, or other

Heat oven to 475°. Generously grease 12 muffin tins or a popover pan. Sift together flour, salt, and sugar. Beat together milk, eggs, and butter; add to flour mixture; beat for a minute or two. Place well-greased muffin tins in hot oven for 3 to 4 minutes or until sizzling hot. Pour batter into hot muffin tins, filling 1/4 full. Sprinkle each with 1 teaspoon cheese and add additional batter to fill 1/2 full; top with remaining cheese. Bake at 475° for 12 minutes; reduce heat to 350° and bake 15 minutes longer. Two or three minutes before the end of the baking time, quickly pierce popovers with a sharp skewer to release steam. Serve popovers hot on a heated plate.

Cheesy Wheat Muffins

Wisconsin Department of Agriculture

This recipe makes great use of Wisconsin products.

1 cup milk
1/3 cup Wisconsin honey
2 teaspoons salt
1/4 cup shortening

3 packages active dry yeast
1/2 cup wheat germ
2 cups whole wheat flour
1 cup Cheddar cheese, finely grated

Scald milk; cool to lukewarm. In a large mixing bowl, blend honey, salt, and shortening. Add lukewarm milk. Sprinkle yeast into mixture and stir to dissolve. Add combined wheat germ and whole wheat flour. Beat well. Fold in Cheddar cheese. Half fill 12 well-greased muffin pan cups. Allow to rise in warm place until cups are full (about 2 hours). Bake in 350° oven for 20 to 25 minutes or until done. Serve hot or split and toast.

Cherie's Door County Cherry Muffins
White Lace Inn, Sturgeon Bay

Muffins:
4 cups flour
1 cup sugar
2 tablespoons baking powder
1 teaspoon cinnamon

3 cups frozen and rinsed Door
   County cherries
1 cup butter, melted
1 cup milk
4 eggs
1 teaspoon vanilla

Topping:
1 cup flour
1/2 cup sugar

1/3 cup butter, softened
1/2 teaspoon cinnamon

Muffins: Combine dry ingredients. In a separate bowl, toss 1 tablespoon of the dry mixture with the cherries. Beat together butter, milk, eggs, and vanilla. Add to dry mixture and mix until well blended. Fold in cherries. Fill well-greased muffin tins 3/4 full. Sprinkle with topping. Bake at 425° for 15 to 20 minutes. Makes 2 dozen.

Topping: Blend all ingredients together. Sprinkle over batter in muffin tins.

Cottage Butter Horns

Wisconsin Milk Marketing Board, Madison, Wisconsin

Horns:
1 cup butter, softened
1 1/2 cups cottage cheese
2 cups flour
1/2 teaspoon salt

Glaze:
1/3 cup butter, melted
2 cups powdered sugar
1 1/2 teaspoons vanilla or lemon extract
2 to 4 tablespoons hot water

Horns: Cream all ingredients. Cover and refrigerate overnight. Divide dough into 3 equal parts. Allow to sit at room temperature until easy to handle. Roll each part into a 10-inch circle. Cut each circle into 12 pie-shaped pieces. Roll up each piece starting at the wide end. Place on lightly greased baking sheets. Bake at 350° for 30 minutes. Cool on a wire rack. Serve plain or frosted with glaze. Makes 36 horns.

Glaze: Blend together butter, sugar, and flavoring. Add enough hot water to make the proper consistency.

Danish Coffee Cake

Donna Justin, Just-N-Trails Bed and Breakfast, Sparta, Wisconsin

This melts in your mouth! There are never leftovers. Also known as Dairy Farmers' Delight.

Cake:
1 cup butter, divided
2 cups flour, divided
1 cup plus 2 tablespoons cold
   water, divided
3 eggs
1 teaspoon vanilla

Frosting:
1 cup powdered sugar
2 tablespoons milk
1 tablespoon butter, softened
1 tablespoon orange marmalade

Cake: Cut 1/2 cup butter into 1 cup flour until the mixture is crumbly; add 2 tablespoons cold water to form a dough. Divide dough in half and roll each half into a circle. Place

55

(continued)

Danish Coffee Cake   *(continued)*

the circles on an 11x15-inch cookie sheet. Combine remaining butter and water in a glass bowl and microwave for about 3 minutes or until boiling. Add remaining flour all at once, stirring until a ball is formed. Beat in eggs one at a time. Add vanilla. Divide mixture in half and spread over the 2 crusts. Bake at 350° for 1 hour. Cool slightly before frosting. Serves 8 to 10.

Frosting: Combine all the ingredients and spread over slightly cooled coffee cake.

Butterfly Violet
Wisconsin State Flower

Favorite Corn Muffins

Wisconsin Milk Marketing Board, Madison, Wisconsin

1 cup all-purpose flour
3/4 cup cornmeal
1/4 cup bran
2 teaspoons baking powder
1 1/2 teaspoons salt

1/2 teaspoon baking soda
1 cup dairy sour cream
2 eggs
1/4 cup honey
1/4 cup butter, melted

Stir dry ingredients together in a large bowl. Beat remaining ingredients together. Add to flour mixture and stir just until evenly moistened. Fill generously buttered muffin cups 3/4 full. Bake at 425° for 15 to 20 minutes. Cool in pan 5 minutes before removing. Serve warm. Makes 12 muffins.

Indian Fried Bread

Lac du Flambeau Chamber of Commerce
Great served plain, rolled in cinnamon and sugar, or with butter and jam.

6 to 8 cups flour, divided	1/2 teaspoon salt
1 tablespoon baking powder	1 1/2 cups lukewarm water
1 teaspoon sugar	shortening for frying

Pour 6 cups flour in a large bowl. Make a well in the middle of the flour. Dissolve baking powder, sugar, and salt in water. Pour mixture into the well. Stir the liquid in the well and the liquid will pick up the appropriate amount of flour. Stir counterclockwise only. Stir until the mixture thickens to a point where it will no longer stir readily and the dough rolls around. With floured hands on a lightly floured surface, knead dough, adding flour until the dough is no longer sticky. *(continued)*

Indian Fried Bread *(continued)*

Return dough to bowl and set aside for 30 to 60 minutes before frying. In a skillet or deep fryer, heat 2 to 3 inches of shortening until hot, about 375°; do not overheat. Cut off a handful of dough, place it on a floured board, and pat into a patty 6 to 8 inches in diameter and 1/3 inch thick. Cut patty into 6 pieces. Slit each of the pieces through the middle. Place the pieces gently into the hot oil and fry until brown on each side. Remove from oil and drain on absorbent paper. Repeat with remaining dough. Serve warm.

Note: Unused flour may be sifted and returned to the flour bin.

Tillie's Blueberry Muffins

Tillie Perkins, Madison, Wisconsin

Tillie baked these muffins for the Hoffman House East Restaurant for more than 25 years.

2 cups sifted flour
1/2 cup sugar
1 tablespoon baking powder
1/2 teaspoon salt

1/4 cup shortening
1 egg
1 cup milk
1 cup blueberries, fresh or frozen

In a large bowl, combine dry ingredients. Cut in shortening until mixture resembles meal. Beat together egg and milk. Add to flour mixture and mix until just blended. Do not overmix. Fold in blueberries. Fill paper-lined muffin tins 2/3 full. Bake at 400° for 15 to 20 minutes. Makes 1 dozen.

Honey Granola

Wisconsin Department of Agriculture

8 cups rolled oats
3 cups unsweetened coconut
1 cup chopped nuts
1/2 cup sunflower seeds
1/2 cup sesame seeds

1/2 cup wheat germ, raw
1 cup butter
2 1/2 cups honey
3 teaspoons cinnamon
2 teaspoons vanilla

In a large bowl, combine oats, coconut, nuts, sunflower seeds, sesame seeds, and wheat germ. In a saucepan, combine butter, honey, cinnamon, and vanilla. Heat just until butter melts. Stir into oat mixture. Mix well. Spoon onto 2 well-greased cookie sheets. Bake 1 sheet at a time at 300° for about 25 minutes or until golden, stirring frequently after 15 minutes. Cool and store in an airtight container. Makes 1 gallon.

Maple Pecan Granola

Kathleen Fredricks
The Stout Trout Bed and Breakfast Inn, Springbrook, Wisconsin

1/3 cup oil
1/3 cup maple syrup
1/3 cup brown sugar
1/2 teaspoon salt

1 tablespoon vanilla
6 cups oatmeal (old fashioned)
1 cup wheat germ
1 cup chopped pecans

Heat oil, maple syrup, brown sugar, and salt over low heat; do not boil. Add vanilla. Mix together oatmeal and wheat germ. Stir in syrup mixture, then mix in pecans. Spread out in shallow pan and bake at 300° for 1/2 hour or until crispy and browned. Stir occasionally. Cool thoroughly and store in a tight container.

Kathleen says, "This is great served with banana."

Maple Whipped Butter

Wisconsin Maple Producers' Council

A special treat on pancakes, French toast, or muffins.

1 cup butter
1 1/2 cups Wisconsin maple syrup

1/4 teaspoon unflavored gelatin
1 teaspoon cold water

Whip butter with an electric mixer until fluffy. Slowly drizzle maple syrup on butter while whipping. Soften gelatin in water, then dissolve over hot water. Cool slightly and gradually add to butter. Mix well. Makes about 2 cups.

Rhubarb-Strawberry Frozen Jam

Penny Dunbar
The Gables Bed & Breakfast, Kewaunee, Wisconsin

This recipe is a favorite. Penny serves it for breakfast and as a topping on cheesecake. Rhubarb is grown on the premises and there is a strawberry farm at the edge of Kewaunee.

4 cups finely-sliced rhubarb
4 cups sugar

3 cups sliced strawberries
1 3-ounce package strawberry gelatin

In a large, non-aluminum kettle, combine rhubarb and sugar; set aside for 3 hours, stirring occasionally. Add strawberries and bring to a boil. Reduce heat and boil for 10 minutes. Remove from heat; add gelatin, and stir until gelatin dissolves. Pour into sterilized containers and cover. When cool, freeze. Makes about 8 cups.

Bicyclist's Delight

Donna Justin, Just-N-Trails, Sparta, Wisconsin
Served to bicyclists and cross-country skiers who like to "carbo load."

1 loaf French bread, cut into
  1-inch slices
8 eggs
4 cups milk
2 teaspoons almond extract
1/4 teaspoon each of nutmeg,
  cinnamon, and mace

Topping:
3/4 cup butter, softened
1 1/3 cups packed brown sugar
3 tablespoons dark corn syrup
1 1/8 cups granola or other natural
  cereal

Arrange bread in a greased 9x13-inch pan. In a blender, combine eggs, milk, and spices. Pour over bread slices. Refrigerate, covered, overnight.
Topping: Mix topping ingredients and spread over the soaked bread slices. Bake at 350° for 1 hour or until puffed and golden. (If using a glass pan reduce heat to 325°). Serve immediately. Serves 8 to 10.

Cottage Cheese Pancakes

1 cup cottage cheese
6 eggs
1/2 cup flour

1/4 cup oil
1/4 cup milk
1/2 teaspoon vanilla

Put all ingredients into a blender. Cover and blend on high speed for 1 minute. Fry in a lightly greased griddle, using 1/4 cup batter for each pancake. Makes 20 pancakes.

Cranberry Pancakes

Add 1/2 cup chopped fresh or frozen cranberries for every cup of flour to your favorite recipe.

German Potato Pancakes

Wisconsin Potato Growers' Auxiliary

Juanita says, "This recipe is great for fish fries. I love mine accompanied by sauerkraut."

2 large potatoes, grated
2 medium-sized onions, grated
1 1/2 tablespoons flour
salt and pepper to taste

1 teaspoon baking powder
2 eggs, beaten
1 tablespoon chopped parsley
butter, bacon grease, or lard for frying

Combine all ingredients except butter, mixing until well blended. Fry about 1/2 cup at a time in butter until golden and crisp. Serves 8.

Note: For a shortcut, cube potatoes and onions; add 1/4 cup milk and use your blender. Be careful not to liquefy.

Spicy Apple Pancakes with Cider Sauce

Ilah M. Sessler,
Jackson Street Inn Bed and Breakfast, Janesville, Wisconsin

Pancakes:

1 cup biscuit mix
1/4 teaspoon cinnamon
2/3 cup milk

1 egg
1 apple, grated

Cider Sauce:

1/2 cup sugar
1 tablespoon cornstarch
1/8 teaspoon cinnamon
1/8 teaspoon nutmeg

1 cup apple cider
1 tablespoon lemon juice
2 tablespoons butter

(continued)

Spicy Apple Pancakes with Cider Sauce   *(continued)*

Pancakes: Beat biscuit mix, cinnamon, milk, and egg together with a rotary mixer until smooth. Stir in apple. Heat a griddle to 325°. Pour about 1/4 cup of batter onto lightly greased griddle and fry until small bubbles form on the surface and the edges are cooked; flip and brown the other side. Place in the oven at 300° until ready to serve. Makes about 1 dozen pancakes.

Cider Sauce: In a saucepan, mix sugar, cornstarch, cinnamon, and nutmeg. Stir in apple cider and lemon juice. Cook, stirring constantly, until mixture thickens and boils. Boil, stirring constantly, for 1 minute. Remove from heat and stir in the butter. Serve over warm pancakes.

Wisconsin Swiss Pancakes

Wisconsin Milk Marketing Board, Madison, Wisconsin

2 cups buttermilk baking mix
1 1/2 cups milk
1/2 cup sour cream
1 egg

1/4 teaspoon nutmeg
6 ounces shredded Wisconsin
    Swiss cheese
sautéed apple slices, optional

Combine all ingredients except cheese and apple slices in a large mixing bowl. Blend at low speed just until ingredients are combined. Stir in cheese. Allow batter to stand while heating griddle to about 375°. Use a scant 1/4 cup batter for each pancake. Pour onto a lightly buttered griddle. Cook until bubbles break on surface and edges are cooked; turn and cook other side until golden. Serve warm with sautéed apple slices. Makes 22 pancakes.

Brewer's Rye Bread

Great served with spreadable cheese, as an appetizer, or with meals.

5 to 6 cups flour
4 cups rye flour
2 cups milk
1 tablespoon salt
1/3 cup dark molasses

1/4 cup margarine
1 1/4 cups beer, at room
 temperature
2 packages active dry yeast
1/2 teaspoon fennel seeds

Combine flours; set aside. Scald milk and stir in salt, molasses, and margarine. Cool to lukewarm. In a warm bowl, combine beer and yeast, stirring until dissolved. Add to milk mixture with fennel seeds and 4 cups of the flour mixture; mix well. Let rise for 30 minutes. Gradually add remaining flour mixture until a stiff dough is formed. Knead 12 minutes. Place dough in a greased bowl and turn to coat. Let rise 45 minutes. Punch down and divide dough in half. Place each half into a greased 5x9-inch loaf pan. Let rise for 50 minutes. Bake at 375° for 45 minutes, or until done. 71

Hi-Protein Multi-Grain Bread

Wisconsin Department of Agriculture

4 to 5 cups flour, divided	1 cup cottage cheese
2 teaspoons salt	1/2 cup honey
2 teaspoons cardamom	1/2 cup egg substitute or 2 eggs
2 packages active dry yeast	1 cup whole-wheat flour
1 cup water	1 cup oatmeal
1/4 cup butter or margarine	1 cup oat bran

In a mixing bowl, place 2 cups flour, salt, cardamom, and yeast; mix well. Heat water, butter, cheese, and honey to 120°. Beat in eggs. Blend with flour mixture. Beat on medium speed for 3 minutes. Mix in, by hand, whole-wheat flour, oatmeal, oat bran, and enough of the remaining flour to make a soft dough. Knead until smooth. Place in a greased bowl, turning to coat. Let rise until doubled in bulk, about 1 hour. Punch dough down and divide in half. Place in 2 greased 5x9-inch loaf pans and let rise again until doubled in bulk. Bake at 350° for 25 minutes or until done. Refrigerate after cooling. Makes 2 loaves.

Kringle

Erma Vesely, Richland Center, Wisconsin

Kringle:

1/2 cake compressed yeast
1/2 cup lukewarm water
1 teaspoon salt
4 cups flour
3 tablespoons sugar

1 cup lard
3 eggs, separated
1 cup lukewarm milk
brown sugar to taste
raisins, and chopped dates, prunes, and/or nuts to taste

Glaze:

1 cup powdered sugar

1 to 2 tablespoons milk
1/2 teaspoon vanilla

73

(continued)

Kringle *(continued)*

In a small bowl, dissolve yeast in water; set aside to proof. In a large bowl, combine salt, flour, and sugar. Cut lard into flour mixture until mixture resembles meal. Beat together egg yolks and milk; add to yeast mixture. Add yeast mixture to flour mixture and mix well. Knead for about 3 minutes, then cover and let rise until doubled, about 1 hour. Divide dough into thirds and roll each into a 9x15-inch strip. Beat egg whites until stiff and spread 1/3 over each strip. Sprinkle with brown sugar, fruit, and/or nuts. Starting from the long end fold 1/3 of a dough strip toward the middle of the strip, then fold the other side over the entire width of the dough, giving each kringle 3 layers. Place kringles on greased baking sheets and let rise for 2 hours. Bake at 350° for 20 minutes or until done. Ice with glaze while still hot. Serves 12.

Glaze: Mix all ingredients together and use to glaze hot kringles.

Rohliky—A Czech Crescent Roll

Evelyn Liska, Hillsboro, Wisconsin

2 cups milk, scalded and cooled
1 cup potato water, reserved
   from boiled potatoes
2 cakes compressed yeast
1/2 cup lukewarm water
9 1/2 cups flour, divided

1 tablespoon salt
1/2 cup sugar
1/2 cup lard
2 eggs, divided, slightly beaten
poppy seeds or sesame seeds,
   optional

Scald milk and set aside to cool; reserve potato water from boiled potatoes. Dissolve yeast in water and set aside to proof. In a large bowl, combine 9 cups flour, salt, and sugar. Cut in lard until the mixture resembles meal. Add milk, potato water, and 1 slightly beaten egg to yeast mixture, then add this mixture to flour mixture. Mix until a dough is formed, adding additional flour as needed.

(continued)

Rohliky *(continued)*

Place in a greased bowl and turn to coat. Cover and let rise until doubled, about 1 1/2 hours. Punch dough down and let rise for 1/2 hour. Divide dough into 5 parts and roll out each part into a circle, about 1/4 inch thick. Cut each circle into 12 pie-shaped wedges. Starting from the wide end, roll each wedge and shape into a crescent on greased baking sheets. Brush rolls with slightly beaten egg and sprinkle with seeds if desired. Let rise for 1/2 hour in a warm place. Bake at 375° for 20 minutes. Makes 5 dozen.

Sour Cream Dill Bread

1 package active dry yeast
1/4 cup lukewarm water
1 cup sour cream
1 egg, beaten
1 tablespoon butter, softened

1/3 cup minced onion
2 tablespoons sugar
1 tablespoon dill seeds
1 tablespoon dill weed
1 teaspoon salt
2 1/2 to 3 cups flour, divided

In a large mixing bowl, dissolve yeast in lukewarm water; let stand 10 minutes or until bubbly. Add sour cream, egg, butter, onion, sugar, dill seeds, dill weed, salt, and 1 cup of flour. Beat until well blended. Gradually add enough flour to make a stiff dough. Knead 8 to 10 minutes or until smooth and elastic. Place in a greased bowl and turn to coat. Cover and let rise for 1 1/2 hours or until doubled. Punch dough down. Let rest 10 minutes. Shape into a loaf and place in a greased 5x9-inch loaf pan. Let rise until almost doubled, about 30 minutes. Bake at 350° for 35 to 40 minutes. Remove from pan and cool on a wire rack.   77

Sour Dough Bread

4 cups all-purpose flour
2 cups rye flour
2 tablespoons caraway seeds
2 tablespoons salt
1 teaspoon sugar

2 packages active dry yeast
1 12-ounce can Malt Liquor beer
  (do not substitute)
3/4 cup water
2 tablespoons butter or margarine

Mix all dry ingredients. Heat beer to lukewarm. Melt shortening in water. Stir liquid ingredients into dry mixture. Stir well. Knead on floured surface; cover and let rise until doubled. Grease 2 loaf pans and sprinkle with cornmeal. Divide dough into 2 loaves; place in pans. Cover and let rise again. Bake at 350° for about 45 minutes.

Stollen

From *Mader's Recipes of Continental Europe*

Mader's Restaurant, Milwaukee, Wisconsin, is famous for its German food special-
ties. Stollen is the traditional Christmas bread of Germany, and there are, perhaps
as many recipes for Stollen *as there are good cooks.*

1 cake compressed yeast
1 cup milk, scalded
4 cups sifted flour
1 cup butter or margarine
1/2 cup sugar
2 eggs

rind of 1/2 lemon, grated
1/2 teaspoon salt
1/4 teaspoon nutmeg
1 cup chopped almonds
1/2 cup raisins

Dissolve yeast in milk that has been scalded and cooled to lukewarm. Stir in 1 cup flour
to make a smooth batter. Let stand in a warm place until light and bubbly. Cream the

79

(continued)

Stollen *(continued)*

butter and sugar together until light and fluffy. Add the eggs, one at a time, beating well after each addition. Add light batter and lemon rind; beat well. Add remaining flour, salt, and nutmeg and stir to a soft dough that can be kneaded, adding more flour, if necessary. Turn out on a lightly floured board and knead until smooth and elastic. Work in nuts and raisins (which have been plumped in brandy). Place in a lightly greased bowl; cover and let rise in a warm place until doubled. Roll out dough into a circle on a lightly floured board and pastry canvas. Brush with melted butter. Press dough in the center with a rolling pin and fold over double into a long loaf. Place on a greased cookie sheet, brush with melted butter, and let double. Bake at 350° for about 40 minutes, or until done. When almost cool, frost with thin powdered sugar icing. Makes 1 large or 2 small Stollens.

Note: Stollen stores well for weeks. It's delectable when sliced thin and toasted.

Swedish Almond Twists

Wisconsin House Stagecoach Inn, Hazel Green, Wisconsin

1 package active dry yeast
1/4 cup lukewarm water
1 cup milk
1 cup plus 3 tablespoons sugar, divided
1/2 cup butter

1 teaspoon salt
3 eggs, beaten
5 to 6 cups flour
4 tablespoons butter, melted
1/2 cup ground almonds

Almond Glaze:
1 cup powdered sugar

1 to 2 tablespoons milk
1/4 teaspoon almond extract

In a small bowl, dissolve yeast in water; set aside to proof. Heat milk to boiling. Remove from heat and stir in 2/3 cup sugar, 1/2 cup butter, and salt. Cool for 20 minutes or until lukewarm.

(continued)

Swedish Almond Twists   *(continued)*

Add yeast mixture to milk mixture with eggs and enough flour to make a smooth dough. On a floured surface, knead for 3 to 5 minutes, adding flour as needed. Place in a greased bowl and turn to coat. Cover and let rise until doubled, about 1 1/4 to 1 1/2 hours. Punch dough down and divide into 2 equal portions. Cover and let rest for 10 minutes. Roll out each portion of the dough into a 12x14-inch rectangle. Spread with melted butter and 1/3 cup of the remaining sugar. Starting with a short end, roll up jellyroll fashion. Seal the seam. Cut each roll crosswise into 12 pieces. Stretch each piece to a 4- to 5-inch length; twist and place on a greased baking sheet, pressing ends down. Sprinkle twists with remaining sugar. Let rise in a warm place until almost doubled, about 1 hour. Bake at 375° for 12 to 15 minutes. Let cool slightly on wire racks, then glaze while warm. Makes 24.

Almond Glaze: Combine all ingredients and glaze warm twists.

Main Dishes
Fish, Meat, Poultry, Eggs, and Cheese

Fish:

Blackened Mississippi River Catfish	84
Grilled Salmon with Dill Sauce and Rice	85
Lake Superior Trout Meunière	86
Wisconsin Fish Boil	87
Wisconsin Fish Fillets Mornay	89

Meats and Poultry:

Beef Balls in Cranberry-Chili Sauce	91
Beer-Batter Fried Chicken	92
Brats 'n' Beer	93
Cornish Pastry	94
Deer Burger Special	96
Duck Stuffed with Oranges and Apples	97
Grilled Honey Apple Chops	98
Grilled Turkey Breast Fillets	99
Sauerbraten	100
Sausage-Stuffed Rouladen with Tomato-Beer Kraut	102
Veal Stew with Dumplings	104

Eggs and Cheese:

Ham and Cheese Bake	106
Ham and Cheese Crêpes	107
New Glarus Cheese and Onion Pie	109
Wisconsin Brie Strata with Fruit Salsa	110
Wisconsin Sausage and Kraut Dinner	111

Blackened Mississippi River Catfish

Zach's Restaurant, Prairie du Chien, Wisconsin

2 5-ounce fresh catfish fillets
1/4 cup butter, melted, divided
1/2 teaspoon onion powder
1/2 teaspoon crushed red pepper
1/2 teaspoon basil
1/4 teaspoon ground white pepper

1/2 teaspoon garlic salt
1/4 teaspoon thyme
1/4 teaspoon black pepper
1/8 teaspoon sage
paprika
lemon slices for garnish

Brush both sides of fish with butter. In a large bowl, combine all the spices except paprika. Coat fish fillet with the seasoning mix. Preheat a cast-iron skillet for 5 minutes or until a drop of water sizzles on it. Add coated fish to skillet. Slowly drizzle 2 teaspoons of the remaining melted butter over the fish. Sprinkle paprika on top of each fillet. Fry for 2 to 3 minutes per side or until blackened and fish flakes easily. Transfer fish to a warm serving platter and garnish with lemon slices. Makes 2 servings.

Grilled Salmon with Dill Sauce and Rice

Rice:
1 tablespoon cooking oil, divided
1/4 cup finely chopped onion
1 carrot, finely chopped
1 stalk celery, finely chopped
2 cups water
1 cup long grain uncooked rice
3 tablespoons lemon juice
1/4 teaspoon salt
1 bay leaf

Dill Sauce:
1/2 teaspoon grated lemon rind
1/4 cup sliced onions
1 8-ounce carton plain lowfat yogurt
1/4 cup snipped fresh dill, or 1
   teaspoon dried dill weed

Fish:
16 ounces fresh or frozen salmon,
   skinned and thawed (4 servings)

To prepare rice: Cook vegetables in oiled skillet for 2 minutes; add remaining ingredients. Cover and simmer 20 minutes. **To prepare dill sauce:** Combine all ingredients; blend half of mixture until smooth. Mix with remaining mixture. **To prepare fish:** Brush salmon with oil; grill over medium-hot coals 4 to 7 minutes each side. Spoon dill sauce onto plate. Top with salmon. Serve with rice.

Lake Superior Trout Meunière
Old Rittenhouse Inn, Bayfield, Wisconsin

4 pounds fresh trout fillets
2 cups milk
1/2 to 3/4 cup flour
1 teaspoon salt

1/2 teaspoon coarsely ground pepper
1/2 teaspoon chopped fresh dill
vegetable oil
4 tablespoons butter
lemon slices and fresh parsley garnish

Rinse fish well under cold running water. Place fish in a shallow pan and cover with milk. Let stand for 30 to 45 minutes. Remove from milk; drain but do not dry. In a large bowl, combine flour, salt, pepper, and dill. Coat fillets one at a time in flour mixture. Pour 1/2 inch of oil into a deep heavy skillet. Heat oil until hot but not smoking and add trout. Fry until golden brown on both sides and fish flakes easily. Transfer fish to a serving platter. Empty skillet and wipe dry with paper toweling. Add butter to skillet and heat until sizzling. Pour butter over trout, then garnish with lemon slices and fresh parsley. Serves 8.

Wisconsin Fish Boil

A Door County fish boil is a must and is served somewhere on the peninsula almost every day of the week during the tourist season. The traditional meal includes fish, potatoes, and onions served with melted butter, rye bread, coleslaw, and cherry pie.

1 cup of salt to each 3 gallons of water

For each person:
several new potatoes, cleaned
  and pierced

several small onions, peeled
1 pound of lake trout or whitefish
1/8 to 1/4 pound of butter, melted

Over an open fire, bring salt water to a boil in a large caldron with strainer. Cut fish into half-pound pieces. Place potatoes into the strainer and boiling water. Build up the fire and boil the potatoes for 10 minutes.

(continued)

Wisconsin Fish Boil   *(continued)*

Add the onions; build up the fire and boil the onions for 7 minutes. Add the fish when the water is boiling strong again. Boil for 9 minutes. Stoke up the fire until the broth boils over. Fish cooks quickly; do not overcook. Drain fish and vegetables. Serve immediately with lots of melted, real butter.

Note: To stage your own kitchen-fish boil, use a steamer kettle. Use 1/2 pound of fish, 1 potato, and 1 onion per person, and much less salt. Skip the boiling over, but melted butter is a must.

Wisconsin Fish Fillets Mornay

1 pound fish fillets
2 tablespoons butter
1/2 teaspoon lemon pepper
2 medium-sized carrots, cut
  into 3-inch julienne strips
1 medium-sized zucchini, cut into
  3-inch julienne strips
1 medium-sized onion, cut into rings

2 3-ounce packages cream cheese
3/4 cup milk
4 ounces shredded Wisconsin
  Swiss cheese
1/4 teaspoon crushed thyme
1/4 teaspoon crushed basil
1 tablespoon white wine, optional
1/4 cup chopped parsley

Place fish in a greased baking dish. Dot with butter and sprinkle with lemon pepper. Bake fish at 350° for 20 to 25 minutes or until fish flakes easily. Meanwhile, cook vegetables in a small amount of water until crisp-tender. *(continued)*

Wisconsin Fish Fillets Mornay   *(continued)*

Drain vegetables and keep warm. Cut cream cheese into cubes. In a saucepan, heat milk and cream cheese over medium heat until cheese melts. Add shredded Swiss cheese, thyme, basil, and wine if used. Heat gently until cheese melts. Place vegetables on a serving platter, top with drained fish fillets, and drizzle with some of the sauce. Garnish with parsley and serve with remaining sauce. Serves 4.

Muskellunge
Wisconsin State Fish

Beef Balls in Cranberry-Chili Sauce

Schneider-Peterson-Hawley Family Recipe, Black River Falls, Wisconsin

1 pound ground beef
1/2 cup bread crumbs
1 egg
1/2 small onion, grated
3/4 teaspoon salt
dash pepper

1/2 teaspoon oregano
1 cup jellied Wisconsin
   cranberry sauce
3/4 cup chili sauce
1/4 cup brown sugar
2 teaspoons lemon juice

Combine the first 7 ingredients and mix well. Shape meat mixture into meatballs—1-inch for appetizers or larger for main dish. Makes about 25 to 30 1-inch meatballs. In a saucepan, combine remaining ingredients and simmer until smooth. Add meatballs. Simmer for 1 hour. Serve hot.

Beer-Batter Fried Chicken

Miller Brewing Company, Milwaukee, Wisconsin

This quantity will serve a group of 12 to 16. It's a crowd pleaser.

1 1/2 cups yellow cornmeal
1 1/2 cups flour
1 1/2 teaspoons salt
3 eggs

3 egg yolks
1/2 cup butter or margarine, melted
1 1/2 cups Lowenbrau beer
18 pounds chicken pieces
oil for deep-frying

Combine and mix cornmeal, flour, salt, eggs, yolks, butter, and beer. Chill at least 30 minutes. Dry chicken pieces; dip into batter to coat completely. Deep-fat fry at 350° until golden brown. Drain and serve immediately.

Note: Beer batter is good also for deep-frying vegetables or shrimp.

Brats 'n' Beer

Roger Gosse, Sheboygan, Wisconsin

Sheboygan is the self-proclaimed bratwurst capital of the world. For a taste of Wisconsin, pick up some bratwurst, American or German potato salad, baked beans, and coleslaw for a proper brat fry.

8 to 10 bratwursts
2 12-ounce bottles Wisconsin beer
4 tablespoons butter

1 large onion, thinly sliced
hard rolls
"fixings" (onion, ketchup, mustard,
    relish, sauerkraut, etc.)

Cook brats on a medium-hot grill; cook and turn frequently for about 30 minutes. In a saucepan, combine beer, butter, and onion; cook slightly to blend flavors, but do not overcook. Keep the beer mixture warm and add the brats for at least 5 minutes before serving. Serve brats on hard rolls with the "works."

Note: Brats are best if kept in the beer mixture for no longer than 30 minutes.

Cornish Pastry

Mary Margaret Endres, Mineral Point, Wisconsin

The lead miners often took individual "pasties" with them for their noonday lunch.

Pastry:
4 cups flour
2 teaspoons salt

1 1/2 cups lard
3/4 cup plus 2 tablespoons cold water
2 eggs

Filling:
2 pounds sirloin steak
6 medium-sized potatoes

6 medium-sized onions
1/2 cup chopped suet
salt and pepper to taste
1/4 cup butter

(continued)

Cornish Pastry   *(continued)*

Pastry: Sift together flour and salt. Cut in lard until the mixture resembles meal. Beat together the water and eggs, then add to the flour mixture. Mix until a dough is formed. Divide the dough in half and roll half the dough into a rectangle to fit a 9 x 15 x 2 1/2-inch pan.
Filling: Cut meat into 1/2-inch cubes. Quarter and slice potatoes and chop the onions. Mix meat and vegetables with suet and season to taste. Place mixture into crust-lined baking dish and dot with butter. Roll out remaining pastry to form a top crust. Seal crust carefully and cut slits in the top. Bake for 20 minutes at 400°. Reduce heat to 350° and continue baking for 1 1/2 hours. Cut into squares. Serves 8.
Note: To make individual pastries (pasties) roll dough into six 9-inch circles; place filling on half of each circle and dot with butter. Moisten edges with water, fold over, and seal tightly. Place on baking sheet and bake at 400° for 15 minutes. Reduce temperature to 350° and bake an additional 45 minutes.

Deer Burger Special

Irene Smetana, Black River Falls, Wisconsin

Black River Falls is often referred to as the "deer capital" of Wisconsin.

1 pound ground venison
1 teaspoon salt
1 1/2 teaspoons horseradish
2 teaspoons prepared mustard

1 1/2 teaspoons Worcestershire sauce
3 tablespoons catsup
1 small onion, minced
1/2 cup soft bread crumbs

Combine all ingredients and shape into patties. Broil 3 inches below source of heat, about 6 minutes each side for large patties; 4 minutes for smaller burgers.

Duck Stuffed with Oranges and Apples

2 prepared-to-cook ducks
salt and pepper to taste
2 oranges, cut into 1/2-inch cubes

2 green apples, unpared, cut into
  1/2-inch cubes
6 strips bacon
juice of 1/2 lemon

Rub the salt and pepper into the ducks. Mix together the oranges and apples and place half in the cavity of each duck. Place ducks in a greased roasting pan and lay 3 strips of bacon over each. Cover and bake in preheated 350° oven for 1 hour. Remove cover and increase baking temperature to 375°; baste with the lemon juice and bake 15 to 20 minutes more. Remove stuffing and bacon before serving.

Grilled Honey Apple Chops

4 6-ounce boneless pork loin chops
1 1/2 cups Wisconsin apple cider
1/4 cup lemon juice

1/4 cup soy sauce
2 tablespoons Wisconsin honey
1 clove garlic, minced
1/4 teaspoon pepper

Place chops in a shallow dish. In a small bowl, combine all the remaining ingredients; mix well. Pour marinade over chops, cover, and refrigerate for 4 to 24 hours. Prepare a covered grill with a drip pan in the center, banked with medium-hot coals. Grill chops for 12 to 15 minutes, turning once, and basting occasionally with marinade.

Note: Chicken also is delicious prepared this way.

Grilled Turkey Breast Fillets

This is a crowd pleaser, even for Thanksgiving. This recipe prepares for about twenty, but is easily adjusted for a smaller group.

20 turkey fillets
1 cup soy sauce
1 cup peanut oil
1 cup cooking sherry

1/4 cup lemon juice
1/4 teaspoon ginger
1/4 teaspoon pepper
1/2 teaspoon minced onion

Place turkey breast fillets in a large flat, non-metal container. Mix together all remaining ingredients and pour over fillets. Cover and marinate, refrigerated, for about 12 hours; turn several times. Grill turkey fillets over medium-low heat for 10 minutes on each side. While grilling, baste frequently with the marinade. The number of servings depends on size of fillets and appetites.

Sauerbraten

Karl Ratzsch's Old World Restaurant, Milwaukee, Wisconsin

1 4-pound boneless rump roast	3/4 cup chopped celery
4 cups water	1/4 teaspoon salt
2 cups red wine vinegar	pinch pepper
2 tablespoons sugar	1 teaspoon mixed pickling spices
1/2 cup chopped onion	2 tablespoons margarine
	1 1/2 cups gingersnap crumbs

Trim all but a thin layer of fat from meat. Place in a large glass bowl. Add water, vinegar, sugar, onion, celery, salt, pepper, and pickling spices, stirring to mix. Cover and refrigerate for 4 to 5 days, turning meat daily. Remove meat from marinade; reserve marinade. Pat meat dry with paper toweling. *(continued)*

Sauerbraten   *(continued)*

In a Dutch oven, brown meat on all sides in margarine. Remove fat from pan and pour marinade over meat. Roast, uncovered, at 350° for 30 minutes. Cover and continue to roast for 2 1/2 to 3 hours longer, or until meat is tender. Remove meat from pan. Strain marinade; remove fat and return marinade to pan. Add gingersnap crumbs and cook until thickened; strain again. Slice meat and serve with gravy. Serves 6 to 8.

Note: Ratzsch's suggests serving with potato pancakes and red cabbage.

Sausage-Stuffed Rouladen
with Tomato-Beer Kraut

Pabst Brewing Company, Milwaukee, Wisconsin

Beer adds a subtle flavor. The alcohol boils off early in the cooking, so this dish may be served to the entire family.

1 beef round steak, cut 1/2 inch thick (about 2 pounds)
1/2 cup flour, divided
6 smoked link sausages
2 tablespoons oil
2 medium-sized onions, sliced
1 can (16 ounces) sauerkraut, rinsed and drained

1 can (16 ounces) tomatoes, undrained
1 can or bottle (12 ounces) beer
2 teaspoons caraway seeds
1 teaspoon salt
1/4 teaspoon pepper

(continued)

Sausage-Stuffed Rouladen with Tomato-Beer Kraut   *(continued)*

Cut beef into 6 serving pieces approximately rectangular in shape. Dredge in 5 tablespoons of flour and pour until as thin as possible on a floured surface. Roll each piece around a sausage. Fasten with wooden picks. In a large skillet, brown meat in oil; set aside. Sauté onion in same skillet until golden. Add sauerkraut, undrained tomatoes, beer, caraway seeds, salt, and pepper. Stir. Add beef rolls. Cover and simmer 1 1/2 to 2 hours or until tender. Transfer meat and vegetables to a serving platter using a slotted spoon. Make paste of remaining flour and a little water; stir into the cooking liquid. Cook, stirring constantly, until thickened. Serve gravy separately. Makes 6 servings.

Note: Venison steaks can be used in place of beef.

Veal Stew with Dumplings

1 pound Wisconsin veal, cut
   into 1-inch cubes
1/4 cup flour
2 tablespoons butter
2 cups hot water
1/2 cup peeled and diced carrots
1/2 cup peeled and diced potatoes

1/4 cup chopped celery
1/4 cup chopped onion
1 bay leaf
1/2 cup green Lima beans or peas
1/2 teaspoon Worcestershire sauce
1/2 teaspoon salt
dash pepper
1 8-ounce can tomato sauce

Dumplings:
1 cup flour
1/2 teaspoon salt

1 1/2 teaspoons baking powder
1/2 cup milk
2 tablespoons butter, melted

(continued)

Veal Stew with Dumplings   *(continued)*

Roll meat in flour. In a large saucepan, brown meat in butter. Add water and simmer for 1 hour. Add remaining ingredients except tomato sauce; simmer another 30 minutes. Add tomato sauce and bring to a boil.

Dumplings: Combine all ingredients and beat with a fork until dough is of soft consistency. Drop tablespoonfuls of dumpling mixture onto the boiling broth. Cover tightly, reduce heat, and simmer for 12 to 15 minutes without lifting the cover. Serves 4 to 5.

Ham and Cheese Bake

Penny Dunbar, The "Gables" Bed and Breakfast, Kewaunee, Wisconsin

12 slices day-old bread, cubed
2 cups diced ham
2 cups shredded Wisconsin
   Cheddar cheese
6 eggs, beaten
3 cups milk

2 teaspoons minced onion
1/2 teaspoon salt
1/2 teaspoon dry mustard
1 10-ounce package cut broccoli,
   cooked and drained
1 teaspoon seasoned salt
paprika to taste

Mix all ingredients except paprika together in a large bowl. Pour into a greased 9x13-inch baking dish. Cover and refrigerate several hours or overnight. To bake, uncover, sprinkle with paprika, and bake at 350° for 50 minutes. Let stand for 10 minutes before cutting. Serves 8 to 10.

Ham and Cheese Crêpes

Juanita suggests that this is an excellent make-ahead brunch entrée.

Crêpes:
2 eggs, slightly beaten
2/3 cup of milk
1/4 cup all-purpose flour
1/4 teaspoon salt
1 teaspoon butter or margarine

Ham and Cheese Filling:
1/2 cup dairy sour cream
3 green onions, finely chopped
1/4 cup Dijon-style mustard
1/4 teaspoon salt
dash of pepper
1 1/2 cups shredded Cheddar cheese
12 ounces thinly sliced cooked ham
1/3 cup fine dry bread crumbs
3 tablespoons butter, melted

(continued)

Ham and Cheese Crêpes *(continued)*

Crêpes: Beat all ingredients except butter in a small bowl until smooth. Refrigerate, covered, for at least 2 hours. Heat butter in a 7-inch skillet or crêpe pan until bubbly. Pour about 3 tablespoons batter into skillet; quickly tilt and rotate skillet to coat bottom evenly. Cook over medium heat until light brown; turn to brown on other side. Stack crêpes and keep warm until ready to fill.

Ham and Cheese Filling: In a bowl, mix sour cream, green onions, mustard, salt, and pepper together.

Assembly: Sprinkle cheese on crêpes; place ham on top of cheese. Spread heaping tablespoon of green onion mixture over all. Roll crêpes and arrange in ungreased baking pan. Mix bread crumbs and melted butter; sprinkle over rolled crêpes. Bake at 350° until golden brown, about 8 to 10 minutes. Serve hot. Serves 2 (6 to 8 crêpes).

Note: For 4 servings use 1 1/2 times the quantities of all ingredients except use 1/4 teaspoon salt in crêpes and filling. For 6 servings, double all ingredients.

New Glarus Cheese and Onion Pie

Wisconsin Milk Marketing Board

1 1/2 cups sliced onions
1 tablespoon butter
4 eggs
1 unbaked 9-inch pie shell
1 1/2 cups half-and-half
1/2 teaspoon salt
1/4 teaspoon nutmeg or to taste
1/8 teaspoon pepper
2 cups shredded Wisconsin Swiss
  or Baby Swiss cheese
1 tablespoon cornstarch

In a medium-sized skillet, sauté onions in butter until transparent, about 5 minutes; set aside. Beat eggs and brush pie shell with a small amount of the eggs. Add half-and-half, salt, nutmeg, and pepper to eggs. Toss cheese with cornstarch; cover bottom of pie shell with onion and cheese. Pour the egg mixture over the cheese and onions. Sprinkle with additional nutmeg if desired. Bake at 400° for 35 to 40 minutes or until set, browned and puffy. Cool slightly. Cut into wedges. Serves 6.

Wisconsin Brie Strata With Fruit Salsa

Wisconsin Milk Marketing Board

butter, softened
8 to 10 slices bread, crusts removed
4 eggs

1 1/2 cups milk
1 teaspoon salt
1 pound Wisconsin Brie, rind removed
paprika

Fruit Salsa:

1 pint Wisconsin fresh strawberries, diced
1 tablespoon Wisconsin honey

1 Wisconsin Anjou pear, cored and diced
1 tablespoon fresh lime juice

Butter one side of each slice of bread. Beat together eggs, milk, and salt. Cube Brie. In a greased 9x9-inch baking pan, place half of the bread slices buttered-side up. Top with half the Brie. Repeat with remaining bread and Brie. Pour the milk mixture over all. Sprinkle with paprika. Let stand for 30 minutes. Bake at 350° for 35 to 40 minutes or until set. Cut into squares and serve with fruit salsa. Serves 6.

Fruit Salsa: Combine all ingredients. Serve at room temperature. Makes 2 cups.

Wisconsin Sausage and Kraut Dinner

2 pounds sauerkraut, drained,
   rinsed
1 medium-sized onion, sliced thin
3 tablespoons sugar
1 tablespoon caraway or dill seeds

4 medium-sized potatoes, scrubbed
   and quartered
1 1/2 pounds smoked Wisconsin
   sausage, cut in serving pieces
1 cup dry white wine or Wisconsin beer

Mix sauerkraut, onion, sugar, and caraway or dill seeds; set aside. In a greased 3-quart casserole, layer potatoes, half of the sauerkraut mixture, the sausage, then the remaining sauerkraut. Pour the wine or beer over all. Cover and bake at 350° for 45 to 60 minutes. If using a slow cooker, cook at a slow setting for 6 to 8 hours. Serves 4 to 6.

Note: Pork chops may be used in place of sausage, but brown well first.

Vegetables and Side Dishes

Beer Cabbage

1 large head cabbage
4 tablespoons butter
1/2 teaspoon salt

2 cups hearty Wisconsin beer; do
    not use light beer
pepper to taste

Remove outer leaves and core from cabbage. Cut head into thick slices. Melt butter in a large skillet. Add cabbage and remaining ingredients. Cook, covered, until beer is absorbed and cabbage is tender, about 30 minutes.

Cabbage Strata

3 cups finely shredded cabbage
1/4 cup mayonnaise
2 tablespoons chopped pimiento
1 tablespoon instant minced onion
1 teaspoon prepared mustard
5 slices soft white bread, buttered
1 cup grated Swiss cheese, divided

1 cup grated Monterey Jack cheese,
  divided
2 eggs
3/4 cup milk
1/3 cup white wine or milk
1 teaspoon salt
1/8 teaspoon pepper

In a large saucepan, cover cabbage with water and bring to a boil; drain. In a small bowl, combine mayonnaise, pimiento, onion, and mustard. Spread this mixture on the bread slices. Quarter bread slices.

(continued)

Cabbage Strata   *(continued)*

Place a layer of bread in a 2-quart, greased casserole; cover with half the cabbage, then half of each cheese. Repeat layers, ending with cheese. Cover and chill. Beat together eggs, milk, wine or milk, salt, and pepper. Store egg mixture in the refrigerator in a covered container for 30 to 45 minutes. After chilling remove egg mixture from refrigerator, shake to mix, and pour over casserole. Bake at 375° for 30 minutes or until puffy and browned. Serve hot. Serves 6 to 8.

Cheese Sauce for Vegetables

Heileman Brewing Company

2 cups grated Cheddar cheese
1 tablespoon butter
1/2 cup Old Style beer
1 teaspoon Worcestershire sauce

1/2 teaspoon salt
1/2 teaspoon dry mustard
dash cayenne pepper

Combine the cheese and butter in the top of a double boiler. Place over hot water until the cheese begins to melt. Gradually add the ale or beer. Stir until smooth. Stir in the Worcestershire sauce, salt, mustard, and cayenne pepper. Makes about 2 1/2 cups.

Note: Delicious with asparagus, broccoli, or hard-cooked eggs.

Corn Custard Casserole

2 cups whole-kernel corn
2 cups milk or half-and-half
2 tablespoons melted butter
1 tablespoon sugar

1/2 teaspoon salt
1/8 teaspoon pepper
3 eggs, beaten

Mix together all ingredients. Pour into a well-greased 1 1/2-quart casserole. Place in a pan of hot water and bake at 350° for 45 minutes, or until the pudding is set. Serves 4.

Note: For variety add grated cheese, chopped vegetables, diced, cooked sausage, or ham.

Cranberry Acorn Squash

Wisconsin Department of Agriculture

4 small acorn squash
1 cup chopped, unpared Wisconsin
apples
1 cup chopped Wisconsin cranberries

1/2 teaspoon grated orange peel
1/2 cup brown sugar
2 tablespoons butter, melted

Cut squash in half lengthwise; remove seeds. Place cut side down in a 9x13-inch baking dish. Bake at 350° for 35 minutes. Turn cut side up. In a small bowl, combine apples, cranberries, orange peel, sugar, and butter. Fill squash with this mixture. Continue baking for 25 minutes or until squash is tender.

Italian Eggplant

1 medium-sized eggplant
salt to taste
1 egg, slightly beaten
1 cup dry bread crumbs
2/3 cup salad oil

1/4 teaspoon pepper
2 tablespoons chopped parsley
1/4 cup grated Parmesan cheese
6 slices mozzarella cheese
1 8-ounce can tomato sauce

Wash eggplant and peel, or not, as desired. Cut in 1/2-inch slices. Sprinkle with salt. Dip each slice in egg, then coat with bread crumbs. Dry on a rack for 2 or 3 minutes. Heat oil, about 1/8 inch depth, in a skillet and brown eggplant slices on both sides. Place browned slices in a shallow, glass baking dish. Sprinkle with the pepper, parsley, and Parmesan cheese; top with the mozzarella cheese slices. Pour tomato sauce over all. Bake at 350° for 20 to 25 minutes. Serves 6.

Kaber's Crock Pot Beans

Kaber's Supper Club, Joan and Jon Kaber, Prairie du Chien, Wisconsin
Boaters and motorists come from far and wide for this wonderful special on the
Saturday night salad bar. Kaber's history dates back to 1932.

3 or 4 cups dried pinto or
   Great Northern beans
2 large cloves garlic, minced
2 small bay leaves
1 teaspoon salt
1/2 pound slab bacon, salt
   pork, or ham
1 medium-sized onion, finely chopped

1 tablespoon butter or margarine
1 medium-sized green pepper, chopped
1 28-ounce can crushed tomatoes
1 cup brown sugar
2 teaspoons chili powder
1/2 teaspoon cumin
2 tablespoons Worcestershire sauce
2 tablespoons Louisiana hot sauce

Wash beans. Combine all ingredients in a standard-sized Crock Pot and fill to rim with water. Set temperature on high and cook for 6 to 7 hours or until done. Serves 12 to 18.

Lo-Cal Potato "Cream Cheese" Casserole

3 medium-sized potatoes, cooked
 and mashed with skim milk
1 4-ounce package Neufchatel
 cheese, softened

1 egg, lightly beaten
2 tablespoons chopped onion
1 tablespoon chopped parsley
paprika

In a large bowl, beat together potatoes and cheese. Stir in egg, onion, and parsley. Spoon into a well-greased, 2-quart baking dish. Sprinkle with paprika. Bake at 400° for 30 minutes or until heated through. (Only 80 calories per serving.) Serves 8.

Microwave Scalloped Potatoes with Cheese Topping

Wisconsin Potato Growers' Auxiliary

1 pound medium-sized potatoes,
   peeled and cut into 1/4-inch slices
1/2 teaspoon salt
3/4 teaspoon Italian herb seasoning

1/8 teaspoon pepper
2 tablespoons butter
1/2 cup water
1/2 teaspoon instant beef bouillon,
   optional

Topping:
1/2 cup grated Cheddar cheese

2 tablespoons grated Parmesan cheese
1/4 teaspoon paprika

(continued)

Microwave Scalloped Potatoes with Cheese Topping *(continued)*

Combine all ingredients except topping in an 8-inch round, glass, covered baking dish. Microwave, covered, for 4 minutes. Stir, cover, and cook 4 more minutes or until potatoes are cooked through.

Topping: In a small bowl, combine topping ingredients and sprinkle over potato mixture. Microwave, uncovered, for 2 minutes. Let stand for 5 minutes before serving. Serve hot. Serves 6.

Sugar Maple

Parmesan Potato Sticks

Beth Hawley, Merrillan, Wisconsin

1/2 cup fine dry bread crumbs
1/2 cup grated Parmesan cheese
1/2 teaspoon salt

1/8 teaspoon pepper
2 pounds Wisconsin russet potatoes
1/2 cup butter, melted

Combine bread crumbs, Parmesan cheese, salt, and pepper; set aside. Peel and quarter potatoes lengthwise. Cut each quarter into thirds lengthwise to make sticks. Roll sticks in the melted butter, then in the crumb mixture. Place sticks on a cookie sheet with sides touching and pour remaining butter over potato sticks. Bake at 400° for 30 to 35 minutes or until done. Serves 6.

Note: Potatoes should be prepared just before using to prevent discoloring.

Sweet-Sour Green Beans

1 cup water
2 cups cut green and/or yellow
  string beans
2 slices bacon
1/2 cup chopped onion

1 tablespoon flour
2 tablespoons sugar
1/4 cup vinegar
1 teaspoon salt
1/4 teaspoon pepper

Cut green beans into 1-inch pieces. Cook in 1 cup water until tender; drain and reserve liquid. In a skillet, fry bacon until crisp; remove bacon and brown onion in bacon fat. Stir in the flour and add the reserved bean cooking liquid, about 3/4 cup. Stir in sugar, vinegar, salt, and pepper and bring to a boil. Add beans and stir gently until heated through. Garnish with crumbled bacon. Serve immediately.

Note: May use canned beans; reserve canning liquid.

Wild Rice Casserole

Marcia Meyer, Lac du Flambeau, Wisconsin

1 onion, chopped
2 6-ounce cans sliced mushrooms
  in butter sauce
2 tablespoons chopped green
  pepper
1 clove garlic, minced
1/2 cup butter

1 cup pecans, chopped
1 cup uncooked Wisconsin wild rice
2 cups chicken broth
1 cup wine
salt and pepper to taste

Sauté onion, mushrooms, green pepper, and garlic in butter until soft. Add pecans and cook 1 minute. Wash rice well and drain. Mix with onion mixture; add broth, wine, and seasoning. Pour into a well-greased, 2-quart casserole. Cover and bake at 350° for 1 1/2 hours. Serves 8.

Wild Rice Dressing

Lac du Flambeau Chamber of Commerce
Excellent dressing for game birds, venison, or domestic fowl.

1 1/2 cups wild rice
4 cups water
1 teaspoon salt
1/4 cup butter

1/2 large onion, shredded
1/4 cup sliced mushrooms
1/4 cup diced celery
1 8-ounce can chicken broth

Wash wild rice and soak in water 3 to 4 hours. Drain and return to pan with tight-fitting lid. Add 4 cups of water and the salt. Heat to boiling; reduce heat and simmer, covered, for 40 to 50 minutes until rice is tender. Melt butter in a frying pan; add onion and sauté until straw colored. Add mushrooms and celery and cook until celery is tender. Add wild rice and broth; season to taste. Mix lightly but thoroughly. Use for stuffing or bake separately. Makes about 6 to 7 cups.

Wisconsin Potato Dumplings

Wisconsin Potato Growers' Auxiliary

This is an authentic Polish specialty, Knedle, *using Wisconsin potatoes.*

2 pounds potatoes, peeled and
   boiled
1 tablespoon butter
1 teaspoon salt

2 cups flour
1 egg
salted boiling water

Mash potatoes with the butter and salt. Cool well. Add flour and egg and mix together well. Add additional flour, if necessary, to make a stiff dough. Divide dough into 3 parts. On a floured surface, roll each part into a 1-inch-thick roll. Cut roll diagonally, making dumplings about 1 1/2 inches long. Drop into salted boiling water; boil until dumplings rise to the top. Remove with a slotted spoon and place on a serving platter. Serve drizzled with lightly browned butter, meat and juices, plain, or with gravies and sauces.

Sweets and Desserts

Apple Cheese Torte

The Trillium Bed and Breakfast, La Farge, Wisconsin

This recipe is a favorite and uses several Wisconsin farm products.

Crust:
1/2 cup butter
1/3 cup sugar
1/4 teaspoon vanilla
1 cup flour

Filling:
8-ounce package cream cheese
1/4 cup sugar
1 egg
1/2 teaspoon vanilla

Topping:
4 cups peeled, sliced Wisconsin
  baking apples
1/2 teaspoon cinnamon
1/3 cup sugar
1/2 cup chopped walnuts
whipped cream, optional

(continued)

Apple Cheese Torte   *(continued)*

Crust: Cream butter, sugar, and vanilla; blend in flour. Spread on bottom and sides of a 9-inch springform pan. Set aside.

Filling: Cream cream cheese and sugar until smooth. Add egg and vanilla. Beat until smooth. Pour over crust.

Topping: Toss together apples, cinnamon, and sugar. Arrange over filling and sprinkle with nuts. Bake at 450° for 10 minutes, then reduce heat to 400° and bake for an additional 25 minutes. Serve cold, garnished with whipped cream if desired. Serves 8 to 12.

Apple Strudel

Helen Jindrick, Hillsboro, Wisconsin

Dough:

3 egg yolks

2 tablespoons warm water

1/2 cup butter, softened, divided

2 cups flour (approximately)

Filling:

4 cups pared, diced apples

1 cup sugar

1 teaspoon cinnamon

1 cup raisins

1 1/2 cups bread crumbs, browned

Dough: Mix egg yolks, water, and 2 tablespoons butter. Gradually add flour until dough can be kneaded. Knead dough until smooth and elastic. Place dough in a covered bowl in a warm place for about 1 hour. Allowing dough to set makes it roll out easily.

132

(continued)

Apple Strudel *(continued)*

Filling: Toss all ingredients together.

Assembly: On a lightly floured surface, roll dough out as thin as possible to a square shape. Spread 2 tablespoons of the softened butter over the dough, then spread the filling. Melt 2 tablespoons of the butter and sprinkle over the filling. Roll up loosely, jellyroll fashion. Brush top with remaining butter. Place on a greased baking sheet or into greased loaf pans and bake at 350° for 1 hour.

Note: Add powdered sugar glaze if desired. Cut diagonally to serve.

Betty's Strawberry Pie

1 quart Wisconsin strawberries,
   divided
3/4 cup water
1 cup sugar
3 tablespoons cornstarch
1 tablespoon lemon juice

1 tablespoon butter
pinch salt
red food coloring, optional
9-inch pie shell, baked
whipped cream for topping

Cut up 1 cup of the strawberries. In a saucepan, combine the cut berries and the water. Cook for about 4 minutes. Add sugar and cornstarch. Cook until clear and thickened. Add lemon juice, butter, salt, and food coloring, if desired; cool. Slice all but a few remaining strawberries and place in cooled pie shell. Pour cooled sauce over strawberries. Refrigerate until ready to serve. Garnish with whipped cream and remaining whole berries. Serves 6 to 8.

Note: May substitute raspberries or peaches.

Bublanina

A Czech sponge cake with baked-in fruit served slightly warm with whipped cream or ice cream.

3 eggs
3/4 cup sugar
1 cup milk
1 3/4 cups flour
1/2 teaspoon salt

3 teaspoons baking powder
4 tablespoons melted butter
3 cups raspberries
1/4 cup sugar

Beat eggs; add sugar gradually and beat until well blended. Beat in milk. Combine flour, salt, and baking powder; add to egg mixture. Beat until smooth. Stir in melted butter. Pour into greased 9x13-inch pan. Sprinkle berries evenly over batter, then sprinkle with sugar. Bake at 375° for 25 minutes.

Note: If using frozen berries, thaw partially and drain juice. May need to add baking time. Pie filling may be used by spooning in rows on top of batter. Makes 12 to 15 servings.

Butter Frosting

1/4 teaspoon salt
1/4 cup flour
1 cup milk

1 cup butter, softened
1 cup sugar
1 teaspoon vanilla

In a saucepan, mix together salt and flour; slowly add milk and cook over medium heat, stirring constantly until thickened. Cool. In a mixing bowl, cream butter and sugar; add vanilla and beat until fluffy. Add milk and flour mixture and beat until frosting reaches a whipped cream consistency.

Note: Juanita says that this frosting is delicious with any cake, especially when served cold.

Buttermilk Pie

Sweet, smooth, and almost irresistible.

1/2 cup butter or margarine, softened	3 eggs
1 cup sugar	1 cup buttermilk
2 tablespoons flour	1 teaspoon vanilla extract
dash of salt	1 9-inch unbaked pie shell

In a mixing bowl cream butter or margarine and sugar until light and fluffy. Mix in the flour and salt. Add eggs, one at a time, and beat until well mixed. Add buttermilk and vanilla and continue beating until well combined. Pour into unbaked pie shell. Bake at 325° for 50 minutes or until knife inserted in center comes out clean. Cool and cut into 8 servings.

Chocolate Potato Torte

2 cups sugar
3/4 cup butter
4 eggs, separated
1 cup buttermilk
1 teaspoon baking soda
2 cups flour
1 teaspoon cinnamon

1 teaspoon nutmeg
1/2 teaspoon ground cloves
1 cup boiled, riced potatoes
4 squares unsweetened chocolate, melted
1 cup chopped walnuts
whipped cream

In a mixing bowl, cream sugar and butter. Add egg yolks and buttermilk. Sift together dry ingredients and add to sugar mixture. Add potatoes, chocolate, and walnuts; mix well. Beat egg whites until stiff and fold into potato mixture. Pour into a greased 9x13-inch baking dish and bake at 350° for 45 to 50 minutes or until done. Serve with whipped cream. Serves 12 to 15.

Cranberry Dessert
Wisconsin Milk Marketing Board

3 cups Wisconsin cranberries
1 1/2 cups sugar
1/2 cup water
2 tablespoons cornstarch
1 cup flour
1/2 cup ground pecans

1/2 cup butter
2 8-ounce packages cream cheese
1 cup powdered sugar
2 tablespoons lemon juice
2 tablespoons grated lemon rind
1 1/2 cups whipping cream, whipped
whipped cream for topping

In a 2-quart saucepan, combine cranberries, sugar, water, and cornstarch. Bring to a boil and cook, stirring constantly, until cranberries pop. Cool. Combine flour and nuts; cut in butter. Press nut mixture into the bottom of a 9x13-inch baking dish. Bake at 350° for 15 minutes; cool. In a large bowl, beat together cream cheese, sugar, lemon juice, and rind. Fold in whipped cream. Spread over crust, then top with cooled cranberry mixture. Chill at least 4 hours. Serve topped with whipped cream.

Cranberry Pie

This recipe was a favorite of Juanita's father, a dairy farmer.

pastry for a double-crust pie
3 cups halved cranberries
1/2 cup water
1 3/4 cups sugar

5 tablespoons flour
1/4 teaspoon salt
1/2 teaspoon almond extract
2 tablespoons butter

Prepare pastry for a double-crust pie. In a saucepan, bring cranberries and water slowly to boiling point. Mix together sugar, flour, and salt and add slowly to the cranberry mixture. Cook on low heat until mixture thickens. Remove from heat and add almond extract. Cool and pour into pastry-lined pie plate. Dot with butter; cover with top crust. Seal and crimp edges. Prick the top crust. Bake at 425° for 35 to 40 minutes.

Note: A lattice-top crust is nice on this pie.

Cranberry Yeast Cake

1/3 cup butter
2/3 cup sugar
2 eggs
1 teaspoon vanilla
2 packages dry yeast
1/2 cup very warm water

1/3 cup nonfat dry milk
2 cups flour, sifted
1/2 teaspoon baking soda
1 cup fresh whole cranberries
1/2 cup chopped pecans
powdered sugar glaze

In a large bowl, cream butter and sugar. Add eggs and vanilla; beat well. In a small bowl, sprinkle yeast in warm water, stirring to dissolve. Stir in dry milk. Add to butter mixture; blend in flour and baking soda. Beat at high speed for 6 minutes. Stir in cranberries and pecans. Cover tightly and refrigerate for 12 to 48 hours. Stir batter down and pour into 2 greased and waxed paper-lined 7 1/2 x 3 1/2-inch loaf pans. Let rise in a warm place for 1 hour. Bake at 350° for 30 to 35 minutes. Remove from pan, cool, and glaze with a powdered sugar glaze.

Cream Cheese Cookies

Vergie Zeman, Melrose, Wisconsin

Dough:

1 cup butter, softened
6 tablespoons sugar

1 1/2 cups flour
3 ounces cream cheese, softened

Topping:

1/4 cup finely ground nuts or
  1 ounce crushed cornflakes

Cut together butter, sugar, and flour; blend in the cream cheese. Chill. Roll teaspoonfuls of dough into balls, then roll balls in nuts or cereal. Flatten slightly on cookie sheet and bake at 350° for 8 to 10 minutes until lightly browned. Makes about 4 dozen.

Note: Vergie prefers using cornflakes.

Finnish Coffee Fingers

The Stagecoach Inn, Hazel Green, Wisconsin

1/2 cup butter
1 teaspoon almond extract
5 tablespoons sugar, divided

1 1/4 cups flour
1 egg white, slightly beaten
1/2 cup finely chopped blanched almonds

In a large bowl, beat together butter and almond extract. Add 2 tablespoons sugar. Gradually beat in the flour. Using a 3/4-inch ball of dough, roll into a 1/4-inch-thick log, about 2 1/2 inches in length. Chill in refrigerator until chilled through and firm. Brush with some egg white and roll in a combination of remaining sugar and almonds; repeat with remaining dough. Bake on an ungreased cookie sheet at 350° for 10 to 12 minutes or until cookies are just golden. Cool on wire racks. Makes about 4 dozen cookies.

Honey Carrot Cake
Wisconsin Department of Agriculture

1/2 cup shortening
1 cup Wisconsin honey
2 eggs
1/2 cup fresh orange juice
1 teaspoon vanilla
2 cups finely grated raw carrots,
   firmly packed

1 cup golden raisins
2 cups sifted flour
1 teaspoon salt
2 teaspoons baking powder
1 teaspoon baking soda
1 1/2 teaspoons cinnamon
1/2 teaspoon nutmeg
1/2 teaspoon ginger

In a large bowl, cream shortening; add honey in a fine stream while mixing. Beat in eggs one at a time. In a small bowl, combine orange juice, vanilla, carrots, and raisins. Sift together dry ingredients, then add to creamed honey mixture alternately with carrot mixture, beating after each addition. Pour into a greased 9x13-inch baking dish. Bake at 350° for 35 to 45 minutes or until done. Cool before cutting.

Note: Pour 1/4 cup honey over warm cake if a glaze is desired.

Leona's Strawberry Shortcake

Juanita recalls that on the farm, strawberry shortcake was served in a large, flat soup bowl. The cake was split and each person was served at least a cup of berries and juice; a pitcher of cream or milk was shared.

2 quarts fresh strawberries
1/2 to 1 cup sugar
1 egg
1/4 cup sugar
1 teaspoon salt

3/4 cup cream
1 1/4 cups sifted flour
2 teaspoons baking powder
whipped cream, optional

Wash, hull, and slice berries. Sprinkle with the sugar and set aside for juice to form. For shortcake: In a mixing bowl, combine remaining ingredients except whipped cream; beat just until smooth, but do not overbeat. Pour batter into a greased pie pan or 8 muffin tin cups. Bake at 375° for 15 to 20 minutes. Cool. Spoon berries over cake and add your favorite topping. Serves 6 to 8.

Mom's Bread Pudding

Leona Zeman, Melrose, Wisconsin

3 or 4 slices semi-dry bread, cubed
2 cups hot milk
1 tablespoon butter
1/4 teaspoon salt
1/2 cup brown sugar

2 eggs, slightly beaten
1/2 teaspoon cinnamon
1/2 teaspoon vanilla
1/2 cup raisins or chopped dates
1/2 cup chopped nuts

Soak bread in milk; add butter, salt, and sugar. Fold in slightly beaten eggs and remaining ingredients. Mix well. Pour into buttered casserole or 9x9-inch baking dish. Bake at 350° for 45 minutes. Serve with cream.

Note: May place baking dish in pan of hot water to steam if desired. May add or substitute apple slices for dried fruit.

Norwegian Fruit Soup

1 cup sugar
1/4 cup tapioca, quick or pearl
6 cups water
2 cups pitted dried prunes

1 cup dried apricots
1 cup raisins
1 3- to 4-inch stick cinnamon
1/4 teaspoon salt
cream (optional)

Combine all ingredients in a saucepan and bring to a boil. Stir until the sugar is dissolved. Lower heat; cover and simmer gently, about 20 minutes, until fruits are tender, but do not cook to a pulp. Cool, then cover and chill thoroughly. If desired, serve with cream to pour or whipped cream. Serves 12.

Note: May choose a variety of fruits according to taste and season. Very nice served in a glass dessert bowl.

Oatmeal Cherry Cookies

Country Ovens, Ltd., P.O. Box 195, Forestville, Wisconsin

1 cup butter, softened
1 cup dark brown sugar
1/2 cup granulated sugar
2 eggs
1 teaspoon vanilla extract
2 cups flour

1/2 teaspoon salt
1/2 teaspoon baking soda
1/2 teaspoon baking powder
1 teaspoon cinnamon
2 cups old fashioned oatmeal, uncooked
1 cup Cherry De-Lites* (dried cherries)

Cream butter and sugars; add eggs and vanilla. Beat until fluffy. Combine flour, salt, baking soda, baking powder, and cinnamon. Add to butter mixture and beat until well blended. Stir in oatmeal and Cherry De-Lites. Drop batter by spoonfuls onto lightly greased cookie sheets and bake at 350° for 12 minutes or until just browned. Let cool on sheets for a few minutes, then remove to racks to cool. Makes 2 dozen.

*Cherry De-Lites are available from Country Ovens. (Four ounces equals 1 cup.)

Old Fashioned Cheesecake

Reminiscent of the cheesecakes sold in the neighborhood bakeries in Milwaukee.

1/2 cup butter, melted, divided
4 graham cracker squares, crushed
1 pound cottage cheese
4 eggs
2 8-ounce packages cream cheese

1 1/2 cups granulated sugar
1/2 cup cornstarch
2 tablespoons lemon juice
1 tablespoon vanilla
2 cups sour cream

Brush the bottom and sides of a 10-inch springform pan lightly with melted butter and dust with graham cracker crumbs. In a blender, combine cottage cheese and eggs; blend until smooth. In a mixing bowl, beat softened cream cheese and sugar together; add all remaining ingredients. Beat until smooth. Pour into prepared pan and bake at 325° until firm, about 70 minutes. Turn oven off and let cake stand in oven for 2 hours with the door closed. Remove, cool, and chill cake. Serves 12.

Note: Freezes well.

Poppy Seed Cake with Custard Filling

Margaret Venske, Stoughton, Wisconsin

2/3 cup poppy seeds
1 cup milk, divided
2/3 cup butter, softened
1 1/2 cups sugar
2 cups sifted cake flour

2 1/2 teaspoons baking powder
1/2 teaspoon salt
1 teaspoon vanilla
4 egg whites

Filling:

2/3 cup sugar
1/3 cup flour
1/4 teaspoon salt

2 cups milk, scalded
4 egg yolks, slightly beaten
1 teaspoon vanilla

Combine poppy seeds and 3/4 cup milk; set aside to soak for about 2 hours. Beat butter until soft; add sugar gradually and cream until fluffy. Combine baking

(continued)

powder, salt, and flour, then resift. Add remaining milk and the vanilla to the poppy seed mixture. Add liquid mixture alternately with the dry ingredients to the butter mixture. Whip egg whites until stiff and fold into the batter. Pour into 2 greased 9-inch-round layer pans and bake at 375° for 20 minutes. Cool on a rack.

Filling: Combine sugar, flour, and salt. Add milk slowly and stir until smooth and thick. In the top of a double boiler, combine milk mixture with slightly beaten egg yolks and cook until thick; stir constantly. Stir in vanilla and cool.

Assembly: Place custard filling between the cooled cake layers; frost with your favorite whipped topping or dust with powdered sugar. Refrigerate until served.

Note: Juanita suggest using butter frosting (p. 136). Cake is also nice baked in a 9x13-inch pan with filling on top and frosted.

Rhubarb Crunch

Betty Schneider, Black River Falls, Wisconsin

Crust:
1 cup flour
Filling:
1 1/2 cups sugar
2 eggs
1/4 cup flour

5 tablespoons powdered sugar
1/2 cup butter

3/4 teaspoon baking powder
1 teaspoon salt
3 cups chopped rhubarb

To make crust: Cream and mix together all ingredients until a soft dough is formed. Press into a 9x9-inch pan and bake at 350° for 15 minutes.
To make filling: Slightly beat sugar and eggs together; stir in flour, baking powder, salt, and chopped rhubarb. Pour over baked crust and bake at 350° for 35 minutes.
Note: Good with ice cream or other creamy topping.

Schaum Torte (German Meringue)

12 egg whites
1 teaspoon cream of tartar

1 teaspoon vanilla
3 cups sugar, sifted

Preheat oven to 450°. Beat egg whites, cream of tartar, and vanilla together until foamy. Continue beating and gradually add sugar. Beat until stiff but not dry. Rinse a 9x13-inch pan with cold water (do not grease pan) before pouring batter in, then place in preheated 450° oven. Immediately reduce heat to 200° and bake for 1 hour. Turn oven off and leave torte in closed oven overnight or until it cools.

For individual torte shells: Spoon mounds of the meringue on a brown paper-lined cookie sheet. Shape an indentation for filling in each shell. Follow same baking directions as for pan-sized. Store in a dry place, but not in an airtight container.

Note: To serve, top each serving with fresh fruit and/or whipped cream or other desired topping. Strawberries are especially recommended.

Strawberry Jams (Cookies)

Mary Huser, Parson's Inn Bed and Breakfast, Glen Haven, Wisconsin

1 cup butter or margarine
2/3 cup sugar
2 eggs, separated
1/2 teaspoon vanilla

1 teaspoon salt
2 cups flour
1 1/2 cups chopped walnuts or pecans
strawberry jam or other jam filling

Cream butter and sugar; blend in egg yolks and vanilla. Sift in dry ingredients. Chill dough for 2 or more hours. Roll dough into small walnut-sized balls; dip in slightly beaten egg whites and roll in nuts. Place on slightly greased baking sheet. Make a thumbprint indent in each and fill each indentation with jam. Bake at 350° for 15 to 18 minutes. Makes about 4 dozen cookies.

Note: Egg whites may need to be slightly beaten again before all cookies are dipped.

Wisconsin Cheese Fudge

Wisconsin Milk Marketing Board, Madison, Wisconsin

1 cup butter, softened
8 ounces pasteurized process
  cheese, cubed
1 1/2 pounds powdered sugar

1/2 cup cocoa
1/2 cup non-fat dry milk
2 teaspoons vanilla
2 cups coarsely chopped nuts

In a large saucepan over medium heat, melt butter and cheese; stir constantly. Remove from heat. Sift together powdered sugar and cocoa; add to cheese mixture. Stir in dry milk, vanilla, and nuts. Pour into a 9x9-inch pan. Chill until firm. Makes 3 pounds.

Sites to See

Apostle Islands, offshore Bayfield, offer "deep-sea" fishing for trout and salmon.

Cave of the Mounds, between Mount Horeb and Blue Mounds, has hundreds of colorful stone formations in the cavern's 14 rooms.

*Circus World Museum, in Baraboo, has a large collection of equipment used by U.S. circuses, including items used by the Ringling brothers. The Ringling brothers started their world-famous circus in Baraboo in 1884. Circus acts are performed daily during the summer.

Door County, on Door Peninsula, a popular vacation spot with many resorts, beaches, fruit orchards, arts and craft shops, and a picturesque countryside.

House on the Rock, near Dodgeville, began as a 22-room house built on top of a huge rock that rises 450 feet. The complex has developed into a popular tourist attraction with a unique museum.

Little Norway, Blue Mounds, was built in 1926 to preserve a Norwegian homestead of the early 1800s.

(continued)

Sites to See *(continued)*

Madeline Island Historical Museum is at LaPoint, once an American fur company trading post and a French trading post.

Madison is the state capital, Wisconsin's second largest city, and home of the University of Wisconsin. Three lakes within the city make Wisconsin's capital city one of the nation's most beautiful.

Milwaukee is Wisconsin's largest city and a leading center of German-American culture. Once a fur trading center, it is now known for manufacturing, its brewing industry, Lake Michigan harbor, museums, fine restaurants, and spirit of *gemütlichkeit* (a German word meaning "good fellowship").

Octagon House and **America's First Kindergarten**, Watertown.

*Old Wade House, Greenbush, includes the Jung Carriage Museum collection of 70 carriages. Built in 1853 as a stagecoach inn.

*Old World Wisconsin, near Eagle, is an outdoor ethnic museum that contains buildings built by Wisconsin immigrants of the 1800s. *(continued)*

Sites to See   *(continued)*

*Pendarvis, Mineral Point, preserved and restored 1830s and 1840s homes built by Cornish immigrants.
*Stonefield Village, Cassville, replica of 1890 village, includes a farm tool museum.
Taliesin, near Spring Green, was the country estate of the American architect Frank Lloyd Wright.
*Villa Louis, on the Mississippi River at Prairie du Chien, was built in 1870 by fur trader Hercules Dousman, one of Wisconsin's first millionaires. This Victorian mansion is furnished with many of the original pieces. The remains of Fort Crawford and a fur trade museum are on the grounds.
Wisconsin Dells is a popular vacation spot where the Wisconsin River has cut a channel 7 miles long and 100 feet deep through soft sandstone, carving many interesting formations. There are boat rides, water shows, and Indian ceremonial dancing plus many other forms of entertainment.

* *Operated by the Wisconsin State Historical Society.*

BOOKS BY MAIL Stocking Stuffers POSTPAID You may mix titles. One book for $10.95; two for $16; three for $23; four for $28; twelve for $75 *(Prices subject to change.)* Please call 1-800-728-9998.

Æbleskiver and More (Danish)
Dandy Dutch Recipes
Dutch Style Recipes
Dear Danish Recipes
Fine Finnish Foods
German Style Recipes
Great German Recipes
Norwegian Recipes
Scandinavian Holiday Recipes
Scandinavian Smorgasbord Recipes
Scandinavian Style Fish and Seafood Recipes
Scandinavian Sweet Treats
Splendid Swedish Recipes
Time-Honored Norwegian Recipes
Waffles, Flapjacks, Pancakes
Slavic Specialties
Pleasing Polish Recipes
Cherished Czech Recipes

Czech & Slovak Kolaches & Sweet Treats
Quality Czech Mushroom Recipes
Quality Dumpling Recipes
Amish Mennonite Recipes & Traditions
American Gothic Cookbook
Recipes from Ireland
Savory Scottish Recipes
Ukrainian Recipes
Tales from Texas Tables
License to Cook Alaska Style
License to Cook Arizona Style
License to Cook Italian Style
License to Cook Iowa Style
License to Cook Minnesota Style
License to Cook New Mexico Style
License to Cook Oregon Style
License to Cook Texas Style
License to Cook Wisconsin Style

PENFIELD BOOKS • 215 BROWN STREET • IOWA CITY, IA 52245-5801 • WWW.PENFIELDBOOKS.COM